Through a
Glass Brightly

Through a Glass Brightly

The Fall and Rise of an Alcoholic

Nick Charles

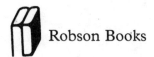 Robson Books

First published in Great Britain in 1998 by Robson Books
Ltd, Bolsover House, 5-6 Clipstone Street, London W1P 8LE

British Library Cataloguing in Publication Data
A catalogue record for this title is available from the British
Library

ISBN 1 86105 222 7

Typeset in 11½/14pt Plantin by
FSH Print & Production Ltd, London
Printed and bound in Great Britain by Butler & Tanner Ltd.,
Frome and London

To Kelly
who knows it all and still loves me

Acknowledgements

I would like to pay tribute to my dear friend Alasdair Barke and thank him for a lifetime's influence.

If there was an award for tolerance, competence and loyalty Teresa Weiler would win it outright; her steadfast belief in me and my written work has been an inspiration.

Nikki de Villiers ran Chaucer Clinic while I scribbled. When my head dropped her now sober smile made a magic pen.

Kenneth Earle is in a league of his own. If a fairer agent exists I have not met him in thirty-nine years connected with the entertainment business.

Denise Halton typed the first full draft and remains one of my dearest friends. Tracey Griffiths worked tirelessly to complete the task.

I would like to thank Des Casement, 'wherever he may be' for buying me my first sober pen.

I would like to thank everyone at Robson Books.

Finally, a huge thank you to everyone not mentioned, past and present, without whose help and support this publication would not have been possible.

If fame and fortune
Are the coins you seek
From the fabled crock of gold,
Have you ever wondered
What lies in wait
At the other end of the rainbow?

Alasdair Barke

1

Crippled for Life

I recall having an interview for a job in Manchester. I do not recall leaving the house. I do recall hiring a car from a nearby garage and pointing it north.

There was the inevitable pub and a girl. Noisy music, flashing lights, a bed, sleep and finally nothing.

I awoke feeling very strange. The sensation was totally unreal. The room was a bedroom I had never seen before, neatly furnished and decorated in many colours. But each colour was peculiarly vivid. It was impossible to describe.

I tried to sit up. Then I realised that I was tied by my wrists and ankles to the four corners of the bed. A cold sweat broke out all over me and a feeling of indescribable fear gripped and paralysed every nerve.

Suddenly, the door opened and the girl from the night before stood waiting. Behind her, a good head and shoulders taller, stood the biggest, ugliest man I had ever seen in my life. The girl was laughing, but the man leered at me with an expression more horrifically evil than the normal mind could imagine. The girl, still laughing, advanced towards the bed. Her voice sounded as if it was amplified by an echo chamber.

Now the man came closer and spoke for the first time. Stark terror, coupled with echo waves, rebounded off the walls. I couldn't hear all the words but the message was only too clear ... she was his wife!

My head was in turmoil. Had he caught me in bed with her? Had she set me up for some insane or perverted game? Then I saw the knife.

The blade was all of twelve inches long and reflected the blues, greens, reds and yellows of the room in flashes of distorted colour. A forward thrust with deadly speed and the knife penetrated my foot. My teeth sank into my tongue and blood mixed with vomit as I strained against my bonds. The pain was excruciating as my tormentor twisted that lethal blade, grinding it against the bones deep within my foot. I prayed for unconsciousness to take over. It did not.

Somehow I retained my faculties, but there was further agony as the cold steel of the weapon was torn from the wicked wound it had created. What had been my right foot was now a soggy mass of raw meat. My head was filled with terrifying sounds, similar to an orchestra playing discords to heighten the tension in a horror movie. My tormentor was shouting and screaming obscenities and I knew more was to follow.

Why, oh why, could I not pass out? Please God! Let me die now. I was pleading for an end to my ordeal in sobbing, anguished cries; begging for a merciful release. Then a saw was produced.

It was an ordinary carpenter's tool, about two and a half feet in length, with sharp teeth. As it made its first, brutal, tearing incision – just below my knee – I realised he was going to amputate my leg. Now I knew that I was going insane, driven mad by the pain and effects of my ordeal. I was blabbering and crying like a demented child. Blood spurted from me with a force that sprayed the room. The thrusts of the saw severed flesh and bone with ease.

I heard a sickening thud as my severed limb hit the floor. My whole body was one searing mass of pain, and I felt my clenched teeth breaking under the terrible pressure as my tormentor continued his surgery on my other leg.

Suddenly, and incredibly, it was over. He was gone and there was no sign of the girl. My arms were free and I was lying on the floor, writhing in agony.

Seeing my chance of escape, I struggled to the door on my bleeding stumps. Then I fell down a carpeted stairway but, somehow, managed to get through the door into the warm morning air.

I crawled, screaming for help, with my raw limbs dragging on the concrete pathway which led to a busy street. I was now surrounded by people and recognised the blue uniform of a policeman. It was then that my earlier prayers were answered and I lapsed into deep unconsciousness.

'Can you tell me something about yourself, young man?'

My eyes were out of focus, but I could make out a white-clad figure beside my bed. I moved my aching body a few inches and rubbed my eyes in an attempt to obtain a little clarity. I could identify some of the surroundings now. It was obviously a hospital ward, and my companion a doctor.

'You had nothing on your person to identify you when you were admitted.' The voice seemed more real than before, and I gazed in its direction.

'Nothing?' My voice was shaky and sounded unfamiliar.

'Only a motor car ignition key.' The white figure had become a man of about forty in a surgical coat.

'My name is Nick Charles ... will I be fitted with wooden legs?' The doctor completely failed to conceal his look of amazement.

'Excuse me, I'll be back in a moment,' he said and walked out of the ward. When he returned he was accompanied by a colleague.

'Now, I am Dr King,' he said, introducing himself, 'and this is Dr Ross who would like to talk to you.'

Ross was a small, dapper man of about fifty years of age and thinning on top.

'Hello, Nick. Would you like to tell me what has been

happening to you?' Both men gazed down expectantly in my direction. My eyes scanned the ward, it was a normal sized room by hospital standards – but somehow different – and I could not quite decide what was wrong.

I was at one end of the ward and, apart from four patients at the other, all the beds were empty. My eyes focused back on the doctors.

'I would have thought that was obvious,' was my reply.

'Well, not altogether,' answered Ross, firmly but gently. 'Could you tell us from the beginning, if you feel well enough?'

He had a point there. I felt lousy. My head was splitting and, God knows, I needed a drink! I was getting withdrawal pains from the booze, or lack of it, and I ached everywhere. I considered the situation; the police would be next on the scene and they would want to know. I decided that the doctors deserved an explanation.

As best as I could remember, I repeated my experiences. Certain parts made me wince and, towards the end, I felt really ill reliving them. When I had finished, there was a short silence and then Dr Ross said. 'Would you like to sit up?'

My reaction was one of amazement so he came over to my bed and turned back the bedclothes. I looked, incredulously, at the human form that was my body stretching out before me ... It was all there, untouched, undamaged and totally functional. My mind was in a turmoil. How? Why? I broke down and wept uncontrollably.

I was immediately sedated. I felt the needle; peace and tranquillity followed and I floated into a deep sleep.

It was some days before I learned the whole truth. I was in a psychiatric hospital, and Dr Ross explained fully his suspicions that I was an alcoholic.

'Your body showed signs of an enormous alcohol presence and I am quite sure that you had been overdosing dramatically, without food, for a long period. The high alcohol blood level on an empty stomach meant you endured something similar to a drug-induced trip.'

'You mean all of that was an hallucination?' I stammered.

4

'A very, very bad one,' said Dr Ross sympathetically.

I lay back on the bed, exhausted. 'It was all those bombs Hitler dropped, my lad – one of them shook up your brains for sure.' My mother's words repeated themselves again and again like a stylus struggling to overcome an obstruction in the groove of an ageing record. Her voice was so clear that I could have been back in my old bedroom at home years before. Mother would yell up the stairs for me to get out of bed while I struggled, under the bedclothes, with the awful withdrawal symptoms from alcohol.

Sweating now, as I had then, I fought the voice that was telling me that my ordeal had only been a bad hallucination. Despite sedation I spent a sleepless night and was always checking that my legs were still there, because I was completely unsure of what constituted reality.

I was aware that there was a thin line between insanity and normality. I thought of it as the silky thread of a spider and, for me, the thread seemed broken. Only as the effects of the alcohol wore off would I begin to cope with the truth that I still had legs... and learn to live with the phantom amputation pains that seemed so real and would haunt me for ever.

Despite my ordeal a more immediate problem faced me. I had to return to my family with a plausible excuse for my disappearance, and to explain the fact that I was still unemployed.

However, my story really started twenty-four years before ...

2

The Start of it All

On December 15th, 1944, a young police officer and his wife were celebrating the birth of their first child, a son. Little did they know, as the years progressed, that their pride, together with that of their daughter born eight years later, would turn to hate, loathing and, above all, shame. They were my parents, she was my sister, I was their first-born.

In the main my childhood was quite normal. However, I was born with one handicap which would affect my whole school-life ... my old man was a copper!

We had moved to a predominantly middle-class town and my first three years at school were uncomplicated. I mixed with children whose parents were in respectable, prominent positions. As I was no different, I was accepted without question. They were a very happy three years and I really do not recall a rainy day.

After three years, the police force transferred my father to another town, situated on the River Severn, west of Birmingham. A few miles away lay a large industrial town. The new school was to prove a very different proposition.

My fellow scholars were mainly working class. As the son of the local police officer, I was destined to spend most of my school days on the outside looking in. I did not wish to be different but, to them, I was. Initially, the naivety which accompanies early childhood prevented my father's occupation from being an immediate problem. Nevertheless I began to develop an inferiority complex rooted in a lack of self-assurance and I realised I was becoming more and more of a 'loner'. In September, 1955, an event occurred that was destined to change the whole course of my life.

Even now – all these years later – I can still recall the smell of freshly cut lawns and feel a gentle summer breeze on my face while sitting on a wall dividing the police station from a side alleyway. The new generation – the teddy boys – were going by. They wore tight, drainpipe trousers, flashy shirts, luminous socks and velvet-flashed, long jackets. As I gazed, transfixed, my thoughts were interrupted by the appearance of Roy.

Every village or small town has a Roy. Young, about twenty, he was full of the exuberance that only comes with youth. Good-looking and forever helpful, Roy was the town's darling, and since recently forming the first skiffle group, a great favourite among the younger set. He noticed me and came over.

He had a guitar around his neck and began to strum and sing one of the latest songs. I was enthralled and when Roy announced that he was going to sell his guitar, I flew indoors to beg my father to buy it for my not-too-distant birthday. The deal was soon settled and I was then the proud owner of Roy's guitar while he went off to buy an engagement ring.

I took to those six strings like a duck takes to water and, as I had always been noted for my singing voice, being an active member of the church and school choir, it seemed only natural that I did my first paid booking, four months later, in short trousers. The 'gig' was at the school canteen in aid of the local football team. I was paid the princely sum of five shillings for fifteen minutes and it was a great success; the beginning of what appeared to be a star-spangled future. That, at least, was what many people thought – including myself!

Before long I was asked to join a group. Those were the days when amplifiers were the exception rather than the rule. If you had an amplifier you were king! Without one, your group had to rely on manpower. Our group may not have had an amplifier, but we had no fewer than ten acoustic guitars, all in line, and we strummed hell out of the strings for greater volume. Also in the line-up was a bass made from a tea chest and – by swapping two old forgotten pairs of my father's police uniform trousers at a second-hand shop – a washboard. We did the occasional booking where we had to travel but, in the main, we played in an annexe to a local pub and soon all the kids were coming along. The pub was quite near the River Severn and the kids would spill out of the annexe and continue dancing on the river banks. They were happy, happy days ...

Over the years I graduated from group to group, getting better all the time. My mind was always set on stardom and I concentrated less and less on my lessons and more and more on music.

Just before leaving school I met Alasdair Barke and his wife who were fairly near neighbours. My younger sister had made close friends with their daughter and was always in and out of the house they had converted from four one-bedroomed workers' cottages. Inside were beams running the whole length of the roof and there was a sitting-room which Alasdair called the 'Den'. It was furnished with second-hand 'club' armchairs and there were books – everywhere!

Alasdair had an old tape recorder and we spent several hours at weekends on recording and playbacks – plus lots of criticism. I think he was the first adult, apart from my parents, to recognise that I had a genuine talent but, looking back, I was a young man in too much of a hurry.

I left school in December, 1959, and, coincidentally, my father retired from the police force at the same time. In September of that year an old man, living in a select part of the village not far from Alasdair Barke, collapsed on to his open living-room fire. He was tragically burned to death and set fire to the house at the same time. The damage to the house was not too bad and, as my father had handled the police side of

8

the case, he saw an opportunity for accommodation on his retirement.

Shortly after moving in, but prior to his retirement, Dad was dragging the river in an attempt to find a suicide victim who had jumped from the bridge. Dragging a waterway was standard procedure to locate a body deemed not to have floated downstream. The boats used were flat-bottomed, police rowing boats. The difficult part arose when the corpse, caught by the drag hooks, had to be lifted into the boat. There were usually three officers aboard, and two would balance the slender craft while the third hauled the deadweight out of the water. My father pulled the lifeless body aboard and, tragically, the strain detached the retina in his right eye. He was in hospital and then on the sick list for about three months. Not a good start to retirement.

My mother was a Black Country woman, born and bred in and around the towns of Lye, Dudley and Brierley Hill. The people were, and still are, fiercely proud and full of passion for things they believe in. Her father had been killed in his early thirties as a result of a coalmining accident when she was only a year old. Despite being widowed with five young children to raise, her mother worked endless hours and eventually married, a delightful man who proposed to her on the doorstep of the small house they would eventually go on to buy together.

Mother idolised me and was proud of everything I achieved, however small. In me she could see no wrong, a devotion she would one day pay for with her life. My father's upbringing, on the other hand, had been quite different. The son of a police superintendent, he became the first police cadet in his county force and as the youngest child he was his mother's favourite. Prior to her marriage, his mother had been Nellie Baskerville, who together with her sister Edith, were the last of their line of the Herefordshire clan who claimed to be one of England's oldest families. Occasionally, during my very early childhood, I recall journeying to Herefordshire with the family to visit some of the remaining distant members of the line. My memory is of them being extremely ancient and I have a recollection of one in a wheelchair who seemed to be near death. To a small child they were awesome and, though of course memories are fashioned by the passage of time, each time I watch a period film featuring nobility it's them I see.

My mother and father met when they both attended a large dinner party thrown by a Midlands industrialist who was a friend of Benjamin, my grandfather on my dad's side. Mother was employed as Nanny to the wealthy family and treated as one of their own. Their union began almost immediately and my childhood was filled with wonderfully grandiose tales of hunt balls and lavish parties.

Our own lives were quite different. Any Baskerville land or money there had been, had long gone. There was one family legend of Grandad Benjamin attempting to win back property on behalf of his wife, the former Nellie Baskerville. The reality was that Grandad Benjamin had a drink problem that led to early death in his middle fifties. Nellie lived out the rest of her life in a council bungalow nursed by Edith Baskerville, her maiden sister. I remember them as being cosy, but poor.

Alice, Grandma on my mother's side, despite coming from a background of poverty, died owning her own property and leaving several thousands of pounds in cash. Mother often pointed out to me that, while Dad had to pay for burials for his family out of his meagre police wages (very low in the 1950s), her mother had paid for her own and left a legacy to all. For his part, and to his credit, Dad confirmed every word and I remember the night he did so as if it were yesterday.

Whenever I went out playing with the band I never drank anything stronger than lemonade with a dash of beer – on this occasion Dad had taken me out for my first real drink. I had three halves of beer and I hated it and told him so. 'Don't worry son,' he had said, 'it's an acquired taste.' I wasn't so sure. It made me sick. Nevertheless the evening went well and we had our first man-to-man chat. He told me of some of the frustrations his parents had suffered as a result of losing the family inheritance and how he came to be a policeman. I remember we both said daft things and wobbled home.

No longer at school, I was now in the workplace – jobs were plentiful in those days and I moved easily from one to the other. I finally secured a position in the textile industry and, for the first time, began to realise what it was like to enjoy a job. During this time I was still actively involved in show-biz as a semi-professional, although working full-time had considerably restricted my activities.

I had been at the new job three months when I bumped into Roy. He was playing again having tired, rather prematurely, of married life. Roy informed me that he had been following my musical career closely through the local press. He mentioned a local group called the Zodiacs who wanted a singer/rhythm player. Having admired the group for a long time, I arranged to meet them. We hit it off immediately and I joined the line-up. This move was to bring about the first big change in my life. Compared with my previous groups, the Zodiacs, for my money, were good professionals even if, officially, their status was semi-professional.

I was sixteen now but still the 'baby' of the band. This was my introduction to a more sophisticated approach to performing music. It was also my introduction to the physical side of boy and girl relationships and the adult social scene.

One night I shall always remember. The group had done a gig about twenty miles from base and we had taken our girlfriends with us; a practice soon to go out of fashion. On returning, we called at the bass guitarist's home for coffee. He had the house to himself, as his parents were away on holiday. Sex at this time was very much a number between five and seven, and I tagged along, quite innocently, with my sixteen-year-old girlfriend. We had been courting for about six months and, apart from heavy petting sessions, nothing savoury or unsavoury, whichever way you look at it, had occurred.

The lights were lowered and we were all smooching to soft ballads in the smoky atmosphere. The boys in the band – Harry (bass), John (lead), Butch (drums), Pete (piano) and myself – were swaying rhythmically with, respectively, Joanne, Sally, Donna, Rita and Margaret. Little did I know, at that time, that our drummer's fiancée of long standing – the glamorous Donna – was destined to become my wife and the mother of my daughter. All I could think of at that time was the happy, pretty teenager in my arms. Tonight was to be my first time.

The Zodiacs stayed together for a year (several auditions and countless bookings spanned this period) and, shortly after the summer holidays, we realised that we could make no further progress together and decided to go our separate ways.

Maggie and I had been together for well over a year now and our relationship was wearing a bit thin. We were still immature and had our eyes on different horizons. After two months, without any musical involvement, I became really moody and made poor Maggie's life a misery.

One Saturday, while shopping, Maggie and I met Pete, my former pianist with the Zodiacs. Maggie had always disliked him, saying that he had a chip on his shoulder. Pete, full of enthusiasm, began to tell us of his intention to turn fully professional at the end of the year and live in London. However, as he had a diary full of bookings, his immediate need was for a singer. Pete was twenty-six, handsome, a smooth talker and a brilliant pianist. He was so talented that success was inevitable.

I easily let Pete talk me into joining him and his brother Dave, who was my age and a useful drummer and we formed a three-piece combo. The trio caused a mild sensation and people travelled to see us from all over the Midlands. We performed in a concert hall next to a large country inn where there was room for two hundred couples to dance and seating for another two hundred and fifty. A measure of our crowd-pulling power was that the doors had to be closed on Friday and Saturday nights at nine o'clock, leaving many disappointed people outside.

Although we were still going out together, I began to see less and less of Maggie as further bookings flooded in. She would come to our Saturday night shows and occasionally on a Sunday, but we were slowly drifting apart. I was very proud to be seen with Maggie especially when onlookers turned their heads, but my deeper feelings had changed. We were now behaving more like brother and sister. It was the beginning of the end.

I was now an essential part of Pete's plans. Christmas was only about six weeks away and Pete and Dave had persuaded me to turn professional. My parents did not like the idea but they realised music was my life and that I had to have my chance.

The following Saturday we were due to play at a wedding reception. The couple in question were keen fans and had booked us for the entertainment at the reception. On the Thursday, prior to the gig, we received a letter and a cheque – the wedding was postponed due to illness. As there was no commitment to cover the cost of the cancellation it was a noble gesture. As it was too late to rebook we decided to have a night out on the town. There were friends we wanted to see before moving to London and this seemed the ideal opportunity.

Pete had a Rolls-Royce. It was a vintage 1920, and a more dilapidated contraption would be difficult to imagine. It had been found on a farm where free-range hens had adopted it as their home. The farmer had estimated its value by giving Pete five pounds to take it away!

That Saturday we set out with twenty gallons in the tank but fully expected to buy more before our return. We started off having a great time at a country pub when, suddenly, I spotted Maggie. She was dressed in a green and white, shirt-waister type dress with full petticoats – highly fashionable at the time. Accompanying her was a tall, good-looking guy. Maggie looked radiantly happy and gazed at him lovingly. I had given up a lot for music – now it was Maggie! The fact that our affair had been on the wane for some time did not ease the hurt. Maggie had not seen me, so, after quickly pointing out the situation to Pete, we left.

At our next port of call we met some old friends from the days of the Zodiacs. One of them was celebrating his twenty-first birthday and we were all invited back to his house for drinks. They had a piano, and my guitar and amplifiers were always located in the boot of the Rolls. Dave went to collect his drums and within twenty minutes of arriving the gear was set up and an enjoyable session was soon in progress.

On impulse, during a break, I went to find the toilet. As I crossed the landing I heard female voices coming from one of the bedrooms and it was impossible to avoid overhearing a remark which came through the half-open door. 'Okay. You have Pete if you want, but I'm having the singer tonight.' It was obvious from her tone that she wasn't talking about a snogging session. I gave a James Cagney shrug and immediately felt pleased at my own nonchalance. Although my only experience had been with Maggie, I was full of self-confidence and looking forward to finding out just who had designs on me.

Returning to the kitchen, I picked up a bottle of brandy that was lying around and swigged a substantial mouthful. The burning sensation was good – all the way down – and I kept smiling at nothing in particular. I felt great, really great. At that moment I could have taken on the whole world, a feeling I would have liked to retain forever ... alcohol was there – and I wasn't aware.

The session was a real swinger. Booze flowed liberally and we were all well under the influence when one of the company suggested a midnight drive. Pete was tucked up in bed with a redhead. Some of the others were in compromising positions and were left to their own devices. That left eight of us packed into a six-seater and heading for a recently completed motorway link. A guy called Brian was driving. Once on the motorway, Brian trod on the accelerator pedal and soon the speedo needle was hovering around eighty.

Everyone was singing and snogging, hair streaming in the wind from the open windows. Faster and faster we went; mile after mile. The car was now maintaining a steady eighty, much to the delight of all aboard. I had a bottle in one hand and my arm around a girl I had never seen before. Everyone had drink of some description, including the driver who was swigging from a bottle of vodka. Suddenly, without any warning, there was a loud bang. A male voice yelled. 'It's a blow out! Steer into the skid!'

Brian had no chance at that speed, especially in his drunken state. The unevenly balanced vehicle was completely out of control. The screams of delight changed to screams of terror. The back of the car seemed to overtake the front, and then it rolled over and over and over ... Bodies were thrown in all directions accompanied by the sickening sound of metal against concrete. Glass splinters showered against my face and hands, and the girls' screams were bloodcurdling above the continuous, awful, tearing sound of ripping metal.

Then it stopped.

Complete silence, except for a gentle crying sound from somewhere within the wreck. I was quite conscious except for an awful giddiness. My legs were wedged under a pile of bodies and something that felt like a seat. Then I heard the sound of trickling water ... No! ...Petrol !!!!

'For God's sake get out of here before we burn to death,' I screamed, remembering a certain film sequence. Then Brian spoke for the first time since the accident. 'I think we are upside down. Can anyone open a door?' A sudden babble of voices followed. Some guy I could not see said his door was jammed ... then there was a click and a burst of fresh air.

Little by little human forms moved and I realised that I was at the bottom of the pile and minutes passed before we were all out. Incredibly, miraculously, no one had been badly injured. One of the girls had an obvious shoulder dislocation and Brian said he thought his arm was broken. The rest of us were a sorry-looking sight, but God had not deserted us that night.

I have never seen a more horrific tangle of wreckage from which so many people had escaped. The car was a total write-off and had finished up near a flyover bridge that spanned a minor road. It was one of the few sections lit by concrete lamp standards and we all gazed in silence at the scene before us. Brian mumbled something about getting to a phone. Mary, the girl with the dislocated shoulder, began to cry as the extreme pain overcame her shock. I told Brian I would get an ambulance and set off across a field to where I could see lights from some distant houses. The frosty surface of the field gave way under my weight and then I was battling through mud. When I arrived at the first house I must have looked terrible. The plump and middle-aged lady who opened the door to me looked startled but, after I had babbled out my story, she let me in and did the necessary phoning. Her husband was sent out to collect the others.

As they arrived it was possible to see what a state everybody was in. Dresses and coats that nobody would wear again, trousers only fit for gardening, and the tear-softened mascara that had turned such pretty faces into hideous masks.

The inevitable statement to the police. Fortunately for everyone, especially Brian, the breathalyser hadn't then been introduced. He was destined to get away, like the rest of us, with a severe lecture.

Shortly afterwards the ambulance arrived and we were taken to hospital. All eight of us were kept in for observation. I slept for the short remainder of the night as soon as my head touched the pillow. When I awoke the next morning, I was aching in every part of my body. Brian, I noticed, was in the bed opposite. His left shoulder and arm were exposed only at the base of the neck and the fingertips. The rest was covered with a plaster cast. Gazing around the room I saw all the familiar male faces from the previous night's near-disaster.

Without really thinking, I got out of bed and made for the nearest toilet. I felt very unsteady and had a terrific headache. The booze had certainly left me with a king-sized hangover and I was feeling very sorry for myself. On my way back a young nurse took her wrath out on me for leaving my bed unaided and without permission. I mumbled an apology and climbed back in.

The morning dragged along slowly and, at eleven-thirty, the doctors started their rounds. When it was my turn I answered the questions honestly and was told that I could leave at once – but to take it easy for a few days. Before leaving, I visited the girls. Mary was feeling better now that her shoulder had been put into place. The others told me that they were being discharged later that day.

Strangely, there had been no visits from the police and my thoughts wandered to my parents. I wondered if they knew, but immediately dismissed the idea. My mother idolised me and would have been at the hospital at once if she had known. I decided to bluff it out and rang home to say how sorry I was for staying out all night. Apart from handing out a rollicking, she told me not to be late for lunch. Incredibly the whole affair was brushed under the carpet. I later found out that Brian's father held an important post in local government.

The following weekend saw all the crowd together again. The accident was discussed in detail. Brian told us that, as no one else was involved or seriously hurt, there would be no case to answer, however as the driver, he had been severely cautioned, and that was indeed the end of the matter.

Although perhaps not, because alcohol had shaped the first disaster on my journey to hell.

3

New Beginnings

The London trip was a complete fiasco. It was a naive attempt at seeking fame, littered with mistakes due to lack of know-how and basic planning. I returned home alone and disillusioned. The first few days were much as I had dreaded. It seemed the entire population of the village had lined up to ask me why?... and how?...and countless other questions. My ego took a severe bruising.

I had been at home two long weeks when I had my first offer to play with a group again. As I was not yet working and needed the money, I accepted. They were not a very efficient outfit and it proved to be a bore, but at least I was keeping my hand in. Then, one Monday morning, I was having breakfast with my family and simultaneously 'breaking the law' by both reading and eating at the table when, staring out at me from the musical paper, was a photograph of Pete with his new band.

Within a month of seeing the photograph they were top of the charts in every country in the world. Pete was a star. I didn't feel bitter, simply numb. I had wild ideas about Pete helping me, but it was not to be.

I left my temporary group and began to see a bit more of my old friend Alasdair Barke. We did a few tapes and I tried various auditions, but to no avail. An uncle took me along for an audition to the television studios in Birmingham. I came close but never quite made it, so the year ended in failure.

In January of the following year, Alasdair suggested that I try for a job as a trainee representative. I had passed my driving test since returning from London and, as I had taken a job working for Roy in his building business and it was a dead end, I decided to try. A letter was drafted out and I began replying to various advertisements.

During this time I continued to earn a little money by driving Roy's pick-up truck to collect building materials and making the occasional call at his bank. Nearby was a ladies' hairdressers' in which I had noticed a certain brunette. She worked as a trainee stylist and I had been a secret admirer for some time.

One day I was doing a small repair job inside the bank and, in the process of bringing in two bags of powdered plaster, we accidentally bumped into each other – just like in a movie. It was not the most romantic of meetings as one of the bags burst on the pavement, liberally covering everything with a pink film of dust. She seemed keen to see the clearing-up operation as an excuse to talk – I was delighted. Then she told me that she had seen me play with my band on various occasions and admired my music. I couldn't remember when or where, but I gallantly stated that I hadn't spoken to her on those occasions because we hadn't been introduced. But now that problem was solved and we arranged to meet the following Saturday.

Her name was Janeen and she was sixteen and five months. I cannot help smiling as I recall how vitally important Janeen made those five months sound. Of course, to a sixteen-year-old, extra months add the maturity they feel is necessary before daring to attempt a grown-up love affair. Every date is, potentially, a possible permanent match! Janeen was a very pretty young lady and, for a time, my guitar met its first serious competition. Not that there was any real conflict because

Janeen loved my kind of music and supported my ambitions.

I had been dating Janeen three nights a week for over a month when I had a reply from one of my applications. It was for a position as a representative and offered me an interview. We were both thrilled and went out for a meal that evening to celebrate. I was driving an old Hillman Minx that my father had given me, a car that played a major role in my life at that time. It was a grey 1954 model and, outwardly, in excellent condition. Under the bonnet, however, it was a vastly different proposition. I have seen qualified mechanics mesmerised – grown men nearly in tears and my father in a daze that could be best described as a state of shock. The car was so totally unreliable it was unbelievable.

No one ever ventured out in the 'Grey Ghost', as it was nicknamed, without being prepared for every eventuality, which if the trip was long enough included an overnight bag. The oil consumption was nearly a match for that of the petrol, and we would often switch garages just to avoid embarrassment. I could never tell how many miles it did to the gallon, as I had pushed it almost as far as it had been driven. Over the months practically everything had been renewed but it still, obstinately, refused to travel any distance without breaking down. There were many adventures involving the 'Grey Ghost'.

The next day I wrote off agreeing to the interview for the position of representative. It was two weeks before I received a reply, giving the time and place, and I wrote back immediately as I was now quite eager to try this alternative to show-biz.

For the interview in Birmingham, I travelled by train, having fleetingly considered the 'Grey Ghost' as a means of transport. This was my first, executive-type interview and it proved to be quite an experience. The interviewers were experts in the process of elimination and, only late on, did I appreciate the double-meaning behind some of the questions. Nevertheless, the majority of my answers must have been correct because, two days later, I was offered and accepted the job. It was thrilling to get this chance and, in only two weeks time, I would travel to Manchester to begin my new career.

The days simply flew by and suddenly there was a tearful Janeen waving me goodbye from the railway station. I had a strange feeling that this new job would prove to be a very crucial move. Although my experience in show business had broadened my outlook, I was still just the country cousin entering the big world of commerce for the first time and, as the train drew away from the platform, I was not to know it was separating me, for ever, from the life I had known.

On my arrival in Manchester, I found the hotel quite easily. It was a five-star hotel and the largest in the city. As I was being shown to my room I quickly decided that this was the way to live – in style!

The following day I reported promptly at nine o'clock to the sales training office and found myself amongst nine other young men who were to be my colleagues. We talked while we were waiting and exchanged what details we already knew about the company.

The first three weeks were spent in sales school. We were taught the fundamentals of merchandise selling in general and the company's products in particular, and within a few days I was completely brainwashed into believing in the company's total superiority. During this early part of the course we had to change hotels and double-up on the sleeping arrangements. As I had already made firm friends with a Yorkshireman called John Barker we agreed to share a room.

After this period of intensive training – both at the school and 'in the field' – we were divided into two groups of five and given a map of Scotland. Each group had half the country to cover. My section covered the whole west coast, north of the Solway Firth and inland as far as Langholm. This huge area was to be covered in only six months.

The plan was to introduce our new brand name into the maximum number of retail shops and stores in the shortest possible time. It proved to be impossible to call on every customer but it wasn't for want of trying. 'Discipline,' said the regional manager, 'is similar to that in Her Majesty's Forces.' For transport we used white mini-vans, marked from end to end with the firm's name and products and, every morning – rain or shine – we paraded in an orderly line to be inspected by our superiors. Company policy demanded forty calls a day, so it was 'all go' from six in the morning till six at night. Despite the discipline, we all found enormous satisfaction in the results we achieved.

If we worked hard we certainly played even harder. I found it easy to identify with the wartime, off-duty drinking exploits of the pilots I had read about, young men thrown together twenty-four hours a day as if with but a short time to live. Every night we went to bed 'well under the influence'. Early morning rising was the occasion for uttering ritual hangover obscenities and, soon, the boozing sessions became a way of life and the highlight of every day was the seven o'clock, off-duty rendezvous in the hotel bar.

One particular evening I arrived earlier than usual to find myself alone except for two delightful young ladies a year or two older than me. I was aware that, as soon as the others arrived, my chances of 'getting lucky' would be seriously diminished as their prowess at 'chatting up' was much more polished than mine. But, to my delight, the next person to arrive was my Yorkshire friend John, a good-looking lad in any company, and his arrival turned the female heads in unison. With a carefully rehearsed and spectacular fall John picked himself up from the floor, stumbled again, and almost unseated one of the girls in his attempt to stay upright. Within minutes we were both chatting away happily to our new acquaintances.

An enjoyable meal was followed by drinks at various pubs until we finally finished up at a late-night country club. During a visit to the gents John informed me that he was already 'on a promise' but according to information received I might find it a little difficult. Shortly afterwards he announced his intention to leave and we all agreed. As the girls lived in opposite directions we said goodnight, and left with our respective partners.

We had travelled a considerable distance since leaving the hotel and I was now completely lost. Much to my surprise I discovered that my companion was equally lost. After driving around for a while we found ourselves heading into open country and darkness. Suddenly I came to a sharp right-hand bend and my headlights picked up a light-coloured van parked off the road. It was John!

Slowing down, I turned left into a side road and then left again in order to double-back. Ahead was a slight rise and, as my headlights slowly swept down from the blackness above, I spotted John's van facing me, about thirty yards away. We were on a rough, semicircular, woodland lay-by. I stopped, turned off the ignition and was about to extinguish the headlights when I spotted a section of naked human anatomy inside John's car. As quickly as it appeared it was gone. Then, suddenly, it reappeared and continued to do so with ever-increasing rapidity. It was fascinating watching John's pale bottom playing peek-a-boo in the headlights. Just then a third vehicle entered the lay-by and I immediately turned off my lights and watched as the other car stopped, lights still blazing. The girl clutched my arm, 'Look, Nick, it's a police car!'

My blood ran cold and my heart went out to John but there was nothing I could do. I was helpless. John was oblivious of anything but the job on hand. I winced painfully as I anticipated what was about to happen. The seconds dragged like hours but the police car remained parked with its lights trained on the Mini's windscreen.

John's staying power was remarkable and his posterior came and went in a piston-like fashion. Then there was a quiver, a final flourish and it disappeared from sight leaving an empty stage. I couldn't stand the tension any longer so I switched on and reversed, without lights, until they were out of sight. Then I turned on the lights and sped gratefully away, with more than a twinge of conscience.

Strangely sober, we found ourselves recognising various landmarks and, in no time, we were at her door and I kissed her a fond goodnight. We had arranged to meet again tomorrow. There were no complaints about the other part of the evening's entertainment and, grinning to myself, I gave it a five-star rating.

When I got back to the hotel the rest of the boys were

drinking in the lounge and telling the usual blue jokes. Half-heartedly I joined them while waiting for John to return. An hour later he entered as if he hadn't a care in the world and immediately ordered a round of drinks. As soon as I could get him on his own I plied him with questions. John didn't seem to know what I was talking about until I unfolded my story. It turned out he had no knowledge of any other car being in the area at the time and I could only assume the police had shared my reaction and allowed discretion the final curtain. John, who had drunk a considerable amount of booze, wouldn't believe my version of the events and, tactfully, I decided not to use my companion as a future witness.

4

Accident-Prone Film Star

The following day was a Friday. We were due to finish early and have the next four days off. The extra holiday was to compensate for the intensive sales drive that would coincide with our first televised commercials. Home would be out-of-bounds for several weeks.

Somewhere in Staffordshire, on that Friday, a man was experiencing his last days on earth. He was to be involved in a car accident from which he would never regain consciousness and six months later he would die. I was to be his executioner.

That Friday we happily parted company and headed southwards in our mini-vans at the start of the long drive home. The journey was tiring but uneventful and, after eight hours behind the wheel, I finally arrived at my parents' house. There was a wonderful welcome home and, after the usual exchange of news over a plate of hastily prepared bacon and eggs, I gratefully retired to my bedroom and slept for the next twelve hours.

I awoke to watery sunlight streaming through the window; there was a feeling of peace, a sense of security. I stared at the patterns on the wallpaper and pondered on how good life could be – sometimes! At that moment there was a knock on the front door. I heard my mother's voice, the front door shutting and then her hurried steps on the stairs. She burst excitedly into my bedroom waving a telegram with one hand and a teacloth with the other. I opened the mustard-coloured envelope and gazed at the words on the cheap paper – RING HEAD OFFICE IMMEDIATELY. I was not sure what to think. I could not recall doing anything bad enough to warrant a telegram but, nevertheless, I had an uneasy feeling that I must have done something wrong.

I pulled on some clothes and rushed downstairs to the telephone. The secretary who answered knew at once why I had called. 'It's in connection with some of our television adverts, Mr Charles. The managing director thinks you might be able to help.' I was speechless. Why should the managing director want my help? The company had such vast resources at its disposal.

'Hold the line, Mr Charles, I'm putting you through to his office.'

'Good morning, Mr Charles. I hope my telegram didn't startle you too much.' His voice sounded relaxed and friendly, not the stern, businesslike manner I remembered from the first day at the training school.

'I would like to see you at my office on Monday morning. The regional manager has told me something of your extensive experience in the entertainment business and we would like you to have a film test with our advertising company with a view to making commercials for television.' I was dumbstruck. I had taken up a career in sales as a second-best to show business and, almost immediately, I was about to be involved in the most exciting project of my life. I managed to blurt out my excited thanks and promised to be at head office first thing on Monday morning. I put the phone down and sat in a daze looking out through the window.

'Nick! Nick! What did he want? What did he say?' My

mother's voice betrayed the Black Country accent that she had forgotten to conceal in her excitement. I put my arm around her slender shoulders and we walked into the kitchen. 'Let me get a drink,' I said, slowly, 'and I'll tell you all about it.'

The larder was next to the kitchen and inside were two large bottles of light ale which I had bought the night before. I uncapped one and told her the whole conversation. Mounting excitement accompanied every word and she insisted I call my father at the office immediately.

Within an hour the three of us were celebrating in our local pub and arranging to continue the celebration that evening. My immediate and future prospects certainly seemed excellent and it wasn't until the early hours of Sunday morning that I finally called it a day.

I didn't wake up until half-past eleven and had to wash and dress at full speed in order not to waste any of the two hours that were lawfully available for the enjoyment of a pre-lunch, Sunday drink.

Reversing out of the drive, I recognised an old friend, Dennis, who lived a few doors away. We only saw each other briefly at weekends. I shouted an invitation. He made an instant decision and, within minutes, we were drinking side by side at the local pub. Dennis had to meet a pal at another pub, six miles away, at about one o'clock. I offered to take him, so we had a couple of drinks and set off to keep the appointment.

The meeting turned into something of a boozy session and, when the bell rang for time, we were all well-oiled. Dennis and I set off home at a fair old speed and we chatted away, enjoying the fresh summer air as it streamed through the open windows. The road was straight and clear and soon the needle was hovering around the seventy mark. Easing my foot off the accelerator I began to negotiate a long downhill stretch that led to the village. Towards the bottom of the hill I knew there was a bad right-hand bend, an infamous accident blackspot. Approaching the bend, I saw two cars coming towards me – one attempting to overtake the other. The overtaking car pulled back in as the gap between us closed – rapidly! Suddenly – completely without warning – when there was only about twenty yards separating us, the second car, again, moved out to overtake.

There was no time to think. For a frozen split-second I was sure I saw the terrified expression on the other driver's face. The sound of impacted metal ballooned in my head, and then nothing.

My first, post-accident recollection was of lying in the road with a warm summer breeze caressing my face and a bright, overhead sun preventing me from focusing my eyes properly. Then a high-pitched scream rent the air. To this day the memory of that sound makes me shudder. I struggled to my knees and then stood up, blinking with disbelieving eyes at the devastation around me. There was glass everywhere. A crushed door lay a yard from where I stood with bits of unrecognisable metal covering the whole area. Someone spoke to me, a policeman I think, and then I saw a stretcher being carried towards an ambulance. Suddenly my legs went from under me as I lost consciousness.

The piercing wail of the ambulance siren brought me round and this time I was inside. The vehicle was moving and, opposite me, was a nurse and an ambulance man bending over a still figure. One of them was holding a drip bottle and, all the time, the terrible, terrible sound of the siren. It was always chilling enough to watch an ambulance making an emergency dash through a town but to be a casualty, and conscious, inside the screaming box!

I must have passed out again because the next thing I remembered was waking up in the hospital ward. A nurse came along, asked how I was, and passed on. I closed my eyes and drifted away...

They kept me in hospital for observation, my only apparent injury was concussion. Dennis had a broken arm and collarbone and there were four injured in the other car. One of the nurses was a former school friend and, after persistent pestering, she told me the driver wasn't expected to live. I felt a deep sadness, I was involved and felt partly responsible.

Concussion can play funny tricks. It took quite some time for my memory to sort itself out and, even then, there were blanks. On the doctor's instructions I stayed in bed for three days. My boss was very understanding and had managed to postpone the filming until I was fully recovered. During that period I had plenty of time to meditate on my involvement. My mind reconstructed the accident a thousand times and each time I saw the other driver's face and the haunting, paralysed expression. I could be certain of one thing: I was on the correct side of the road at the moment of impact. That knowledge helped me a great deal. If I had been going more slowly, could the accident have been avoided? But why, having decided against overtaking once, did the other driver pull out again, at the last minute? Unfortunately, all the questions couldn't undo the tragedy.

Soon I was up and about and, just a week after the accident, I was filming – on location – in Nottingham. The film crew were all professionals and I was sometimes overawed by their conversation, particularly when they were relaxing in the pub and discussing previous assignments with well-known celebrities.

The filming lasted six weeks and it was a marvellous experience. Going back to the selling side of my job seemed a complete anticlimax. Deep down I knew that it would not be long before I was back on the road with a band again. It was not that I disliked selling, but entertaining was in my blood and I had a full eight pints of musical ambition.

Shortly after my return, I was transferred to Glasgow and given another large territory. Several weeks had now passed since the accident and my confidence was almost back to normal. One evening I was driving back to the hotel in a torrential rainstorm. It was two hours before lighting up but the dark rainclouds had reduced visibility considerably. With the windscreen wipers barely able to cope I realised I was travelling too fast and had started to slow down when the steering wheel was torn from my grasp and the van began to veer wildly. It was a front-wheel blow-out! I tried to correct the skid but the wheels hit the off-side kerb and the van was forced onto its side. I was thrown about like a rag doll until finally, with a crash, the van came to a stop. It was still on its side, but I couldn't tell the front from the back. A dazed glance suggested the back doors had been ripped off. I crawled through the gaping hole and staggered, drenched from the rain towards a tree for support. As I looked back, my head clearing, I realised that the body of the van was on the central reservation and the hole that I had assumed to be the back was, in fact, the front. The rest, which had been torn off, was about a hundred yards away.

The transition from a warm, comfortable driving seat to standing, bruised and battered and holding on to a tree in a storm, is not to be recommended; but it might have been worse... another car could have been involved or I could have been badly injured or just plain dead.

Facing the consequences at head office was not easy but, as I was top salesman, they gave me my third van in four months. The company obviously still rated my contribution higher than the cost of their vehicles; but I was not yet at the end of my motoring mayhem.

A week later my new van was parked outside a shop when a lorry turned it into a sardine can. Only three weeks after that came the final crunch in my incredible relationship with the scrap-metal industry. I hit two parked cars in the early hours of the morning as a result of having too much to drink and fractured my skull in two places. Elsewhere there were enough stitches to make me look like a patchwork quilt and I shall take the scars to my grave. Thus I joined the ranks of unemployed salesmen; but fate decided that some good should accrue.

After a period of convalescence I returned to the company's head office to hand in some papers. On my way home I met a group of fellow-musicians who were returning from a booking in Manchester. They were all Liverpool lads, living in Birmingham. Over a drink they mentioned that they needed a temporary singer. As a Liverpool group they could get bookings without an audition (the Beatles were riding high in the charts) and they had more than their share of professional engagements. I agreed to meet them the following week and arrived home feeling a whole lot better.

5

Merry-go-round

No job – no company car! I was completely lost without wheels and totally fed up with public transport.

Janeen and I spent more and more time together and the conversation occasionally came around to marriage. We had been dating for about twelve months and were seeing each other practically every night. One evening we simply decided to become engaged. I was all for it, after Janeen had done most of the pushing but, as I was temporarily out of work, we decided to delay the announcement until I had a full-time job.

We didn't have to wait long. I had heard nothing for three weeks after my audition with the Birmingham-based Liverpool group. Then ten days before the 'engagement' came their offer of four bookings per week and, with the same post, confirmation of a job. The job was through one of Janeen's connections at the shop. I had been interviewed for the position of salesman with one of the world's largest manufacturers of ladies' hairdressing preparations. I accepted both offers!

It was impossible, however, to give both worlds my full attention; there were simply not enough hours in the day. But

I found a way around the problem. As a representative is largely his own boss, I was able to organise my calls so that I finished within a reasonable distance of the venue with the band. Soon I was singing seven nights a week and struggling to get out of bed by ten o'clock in the morning. Luckily I possessed a natural ability to sell and, although the company never reaped the full rewards of a complete day's work, I did enough to retain my position.

Some days I felt dreadful. Morning hangovers and an exhausting sixteen-hour day were taking their toll. Then I found the magic formula!

One morning I awoke feeling particularly 'down' and was groping in my pockets, looking for the car keys, when my fingers came into contact with a small bottle. I remembered buying a miniature brandy the night before. The bottle had been intended for Janeen's collection but now I had a better idea, a cup of hot tea liberally laced with the brandy. I sat down with a copy of the morning paper and, as the liquid burned its way down to my stomach, I immediately felt better. When I had finished the cup I felt terrific and made a mental note to keep a bottle handy... always!

Janeen and I continued to see a lot of each other although quite often she had to make her own way to see the band. Dad was marvellous. When the car wasn't in dock he frequently drove miles out of his way in order that we could be together. I was getting some rave reviews which I felt had been earned and my faithful morning brandy was helping me to keep going. But Janeen couldn't be expected to come to all the gigs. Dad's car started to show its age and Janeen and I were seeing less and less of each other.

In the late summer I had an experience that at the time I felt I had taken in my stride. I have wondered since if in fact it may have had greater significance. It was a Saturday morning and I had taken Janeen to the local shopping centre. As I turned off the ignition Janeen told me, without any emotion, that she didn't want to see me any more, and she didn't wait for a reply. The diamond ring, which had cost me a month's salary, lay on the seat. The sound of the door closing echoed and re-echoed in my ears. There was no melodrama. The whole sequence only lasted seconds. I remember sitting there for a long time. I did not feel hurt or sad. I didn't feel anything! If Janeen had reappeared, laughing at the joke, I am sure we would have gone shopping as planned without giving it another thought. The whole business had been so matter-of-fact. Nearly a year had passed since my appointment with the hairdressing manufacturers and my 'double' life with the band. I was aware that we had been unable to spend any real time together during the previous months and realised that we had been drifting apart. I started the engine and drove slowly away in the direction of Birmingham.

Half an hour later I pulled into the car park of a small public house. I drank a lot of beer and emerged with a bottle of brandy, which I stowed into the glove compartment, and drove off. By mid-afternoon, sitting in the car parked by the river, I finished the bottle and fell asleep – completely drunk.

When I awoke, the sun was still shining and I had a sudden cramp that was so bad I cried out in pain when I tried to move. I felt indescribable, it was my first major hangover. My eyes could not focus and there was a foul taste in my mouth. Staggering out of the car I tripped and fell, sprawling full-length on the grass. I lay for some time unable to move or think properly, and then forced myself into a sitting position. Torturing my limbs into an upright stance, I leaned forward and propelled my legs into motion. In this fashion, taking deep breaths as I moved, I managed to get all my joints working again; but it took over half an hour to feel in any way human.

Retracing my steps to the car I had an uneasy feeling. Getting in behind the wheel I turned on the ignition and pressed the starter. My suspicions were confirmed, the engine was stone cold and needed full choke. I didn't have a watch, but somehow I knew that my drunken stupor had taken me through Saturday and into Sunday!

Driving home, I was worried about my parents' reaction, but I need not have bothered. Mother was very sympathetic when she heard about the broken engagement and everything else was forgotten. I am sure that the break with Janeen could have been patched up, but I was young and contrary and refused to make contact.

Time passed but despite those sixteen-hour days I began to miss Janeen. We had bought a number of 'bottom drawer' items and I secretly hoped she would come to collect them, so that we could meet, but she never called and so it turned out to be the end of an era.

Two weeks later my contract with the group ended and, for the first time, I gave the company my undivided attention. The hairdressing profession seemed to attract more than its fair share of pretty young ladies, which was some consolation for my recent loss.

In late November the company arranged for various competitions to be held throughout the country and most of the larger salons were taking part. A new girlfriend, who had a large salon in South Staffordshire, decided to enter. She asked me if I knew of any models with a good head of hair. I gave her problem some thought and remembered that Butch – my former drummer with the Zodiacs – had become engaged to Donna who, apart from having marvellous hair, was also a part-time model. I did a bit of detective work and telephoned one Monday morning. Donna appeared both surprised and delighted to hear from me and we spent the first fifteen minutes of our conversation talking about old times, and I learned that she was no longer engaged to Butch. Finally I got round to the reason for the phone call and she seemed very interested. We arranged to meet the following evening in order to introduce her to my girlfriend.

That evening I washed and dressed with an unusual tingle of excitement and arrived at the meeting place ten minutes early. When I saw Donna she took my breath away. For me she had grace, poise, elegant beauty and a perfect sense of humour. My eyes never left her and my heart was full of love and romance – modelling and hairdressing were forgotten.

I saw her as the most beautiful girl in town, a room would

stop when she entered. It was like being with someone famous, I can still recall the buzz.

She agreed to marry me. The fact that she had the pick of the pack made her choice even more bizarre, summed up best perhaps by 17th-century writer Blaise Pascal. 'The heart has its reasons which reason knows nothing of.'

From a religious point of view there had been much objection from my family, much help and assistance from hers and we subsequently married and had a daughter almost immediately.

She had first met and got to know me when I was fifteen years of age and living in another world, a world when I had been free of alcohol. She soon discovered this was a different man and one in whom there were severe character defects. A blacker soul appeared with my constant drinking. Alarming switches occurred between my normal self and the frightened remorseful person that emerged each morning, perspiring and shaking in alcoholic withdrawal.

For my part, I was simply bewildered. My mother said I needed psychiatric treatment but she was the only one who suggested that there might be something wrong in my world. For the most part I was dismissed as a bad egg capable of extorting money with lies, living in a make-believe world and concocting unbelievable imaginings, the intensity of which depended on the amount of alcohol I had consumed.

By the time we had been married six years, I was unemployable and twenty-seven years of age. Donna, for whom I have only pity, endured a life of torment and humiliation in front of family, friends and frequently strangers, to say nothing of degradation and extreme poverty. Had it not been for the money and furniture her mother, a delightful Irish woman for whom I have only admiration, had provided we would have had no home at all. In the beginning, the prospect that her daughter had found an apparently excellent partner must have seemed heaven to this staunch Catholic lady – it turned into hell on earth.

There had to be a day of judgement. It came after my return

home from the job interview in Manchester and my hallucination nightmare. Donna was a good worker, a good mother, in fact a good woman and she could see further than a drunken husband.

With hindsight I think she decided to seek legal advice because one day, unexpectedly, I received a letter from the council to say no one was paying the rent. Mother-in-law had pulled the plug.

6

Eviction

The eviction notice arrived one sunny August day. It was Worcestershire County Council's reaction to me spending all the household income, plus whatever I could beg or borrow at the pub or off-licence. Close behind came a social worker who could not believe her ears at the insane ramblings (including a chat-up line) from Mr Hyde. She sent for reinforcements.

They arrived, were several in number and gave up on me, preferring to deal with Donna. Donna told me confidentially that a plan had been hatched. It was that I would sign the house over to her and she, as new tenant, would be able to start from scratch with the debt wiped clean. I did so of course, it was the obvious thing to do. Naturally, I would have to leave temporarily as part of the masquerade but could return after three or four days.

'Daddy, please don't go.'

The tears streamed down her tiny face as a father who, through a four year old's eyes, could do no wrong was seemingly disappearing for ever.

'I'm only going for three or four days. Look I'm only taking two shirts and a spare pair of trousers.'

The tears abated, she thought there was no reason to cry after all. Daddy would return soon, she thought, she would hear his key rattle in the door in the familiar way. But it was not to be, for the locks were changed and it would be twenty years before we met again as strangers.

7

Further Symptoms

Days became weeks then months, time had no dimension or construction. Various friends put me up briefly, but I soon wore out my welcome. Two years passed in little more than semi-consciousness. Alcoholism is a progressive illness and the progression is as painful as it is indefinable.

A second marriage followed that I saw only through the bottom of a glass, and it ended as abruptly as it began.

After a period of living rough, and confusion and suffering, I found myself alone and friendless in the town where I was born.

I longed to knock on the doors of various relatives but shame prevented me. Instead I walked to the church where my beloved mother and father were married, where I was christened and where my grandparents lay buried in the churchyard.

I was somewhat surprised to find the door open and I entered the peace and calm of the church and began wondering if there really was a God.

I sat in a pew looking up at the inevitable stained-glass

window of the crucifixion and thought of the hundreds of services I had attended elsewhere as a choirboy. It seemed to me I had given a lot to God and he in return had given nothing. If he existed, all he had brought me was pain, suffering and bad luck – none of which I deserved. Seemed to me that Job had had it easy, either that or JC in his wisdom had decided it was about time somebody had it worse! Better hedge my bets and pray anyway!

'If there's a God please help me to find a job as a live-in barman!'

I got up and walked to the aisle and looked down its full length to the altar. My parents had walked down here on their wedding day. I leant on the font for support; someone had held me here while I was christened.

I remembered the story that I had pissed on one of my relations. They and everyone else had got their own back, and they'd dumped on me ever since. God, I knew how the innocent man found guilty felt!

There was a heavy leather-bound visitors' book on the lectern. Foolishly I looked back to the beginning, at least two hundred pages, in an effort to find my parents' signatures – it was dated recently – must be a lot of visitors I thought, what a bloody waste of paper.

I searched for a pen, some Christian had nicked the one that was supposed to be on the end of the string. I found one in a cupboard marked 'Private' and wrote words I would one day read again.

8

The Long Sunday Walk

The locality was noted for its sandstone and caves; I chose one for shelter. Days passed in an alcoholic haze. I had no desire for food, somehow I had retained enough money to stockpile my drink and this kept my appetite at bay.

At one stage I awoke, with no knowledge of time, just an enormous overwhelming hunger; nothing could be done, I had no money. I racked my brain for a solution, feeling very ill and so weak that I had difficulty in standing. The cave went round like the arms of an old windmill, my lungs and stomach ached from the strain of vomiting and the blood in my head forced a pressure behind my eyes.

I could not live with normal people, in normal society. I had hoped that this last bender would end in death and therefore stop the pain and suffering. Perhaps I could find a way, nearby was a river and occasionally I heard a train. A train meant a railway line, perhaps that was the way. The main road was only a short distance away, perhaps a mile, an easy walk for anyone in normal health but, for me, an Everest.

I had now decided, quite dispassionately, on a place to end

my life, a stretch of railway line – all I had to do was get there! I stumbled and finally dragged myself to within half a mile of the main road. There was a small farm nearby and I took refuge in an outhouse near a large barn. My one desire was to avoid discovery. I lay under some old coats in a corner of a small building – almost too frightened to move. I guessed it was late afternoon and I tried for a long time to get to sleep. Eventually I dozed off, but there were horrible dreams that kept waking me. Finally I did find some sleep, or perhaps it was simply unconsciousness brought on by weakness and exhaustion. I was convinced that I was on the borderline separating sanity from total madness.

It was probably the following day when I found the strength to move from my resting-place. The only thing I can recall is the awful sensation of knowing I was terribly ill. The lack of food and major weight loss, combined with the ghastly effects of withdrawal, cannot be easily described. Every step I took was a tremendous feat of concentration and physical effort. Now I had only one thought, the pain of living had to end. No longer could I take the physical and psychological battering. No more waking up to a world that I was unable to cope with. There had to be an end to sweating away the withdrawal and the agoraphobic-type fear implanted in my brain by the effects of my alcoholic addiction.

My immediate concern when making my painful journey towards the railway line was that the police might stop me.

By now I had no idea what time it was or even the day or the month. I did not care, my only goal was to lie down across the railway line that seemed a thousand miles away. After covering a fraction of the distance, I rested against a wall that formed part of a viaduct carrying the railway line above the road. It was then that my confused brain advised a change of plan. Instead of walking all the way to where the line was easily accessible, all I had to do was scale a four-foot fence and then, somehow, climb the embankment to the line above. My brain was remembering a fit body, now it was a vastly different proposition.

Despite everything, I decided to make the attempt. One

compelling advantage was that no one would see me and I would have as much time as I needed to fulfil my dreadful commitment.

On reaching the summit I was completely exhausted and retched again and again. My feeble frame felt as if it had scaled a mountain. It was a further half-hour before I was able to crawl the final five yards and place my head, in position, across the cold steel lines. I closed my eyes and lay still. The cold morning air chilled my face and hands and my mind was empty of thoughts and completely devoid of fear.

A period of time elapsed – how long I shall never know – and I was awake. I felt very strange and was unable to concentrate or focus my eyes. Slowly some of my faculties returned and my brain sent messages to my arms and legs, but they failed to respond. I continued to lie in the same position, puzzled by my inability to move my limbs, and seemingly locked in a period of timeless mystery. But somehow life returned and, very slowly, I was able to move my frozen feet and then my elbows forced my body into a sitting position. Struggling shakily to my feet, numbed from head to toes, I was quite unable to put my thoughts into any semblance of order. I stumbled, hesitantly, down the line in the direction of the railway station, wondering why I was still alive.

I must have been unconscious for a long time, so the absence of trains was inexplicable. Painfully, yard by yard, my aching body drew closer to the station which was strangely deserted. My eyesight was blurred and I found myself wondering if my sight was going to be permanently affected... but then dismissed it from my mind as the least of my present problems. The concrete rise which led to the platform loomed in front of me and, somehow, I made it to the top and collapsed on to a passenger bench. I sat for a long time staring at the huge board in front of me on the opposite platform; slowly the words came into focus.

AS FROM MARCH 1st NO PASSENGER TRAINS WILL PASS THROUGH THIS STATION ON SUNDAYS AND IT WILL BE CLOSED TO THE PUBLIC

It was fully five minutes before the significance sank into my numbed brain. My survival had an explanation – today must be Sunday! Quietly and perfectly clearly without any blinding light or voices from the sky, I perceived that there must be a purpose to life and a reason for living. For the first time in years I had a real desire to live; to make something out of the ashes that remained of the potential I had once shown. But where to begin? No one remained loyal among my relatives or friends and I had no idea where to turn for help. From somewhere amongst the debris of my mind came a name – 'Samaritans'. I clung to that name as I walked slowly along the platform, repeating it over and over again. Behind me the railway line curved back, silently, into my past.

9

Good Deed for the Day

Just outside the station was a telephone box and the Samaritans' number was printed on a small card by the receiver. Despite the early hour, a friendly male voice answered and I explained something of my story and how I was completely desperate...

'Obviously we can help you, but there is very little we can do until Monday morning.'

'But I don't think I can spend another night out in the open.'

'Isn't there anyone who could take you in for one night if you tell them we are going to help on Monday morning?'

'No! No one wants to know.'

'Have a good think, there must be someone.'

I realised the complete futility of continuing the conversation. The well-meaning man could not see me – could not fully understand how I felt. Finally I made an excuse and said that I would try and think of somebody. Hoping that I could remember the address he had given me until the following morning, I walked slowly from the phone box and back towards the station. There was a railway workers' hut I knew of that was the only place I could think of to spend the rest of the day and night, the journey by road was far too long for me in my present condition, so I decided to go back along the railway line. I had to rest, often, as my limbs felt as if they were shackled by heavy, invisible irons, and the uneven surface of the track did nothing to help. The regular wooden sleepers – with their stone chippings in between – were an appalling obstacle for my fatigued body. Occasionally I felt a mild excitement at the prospect of rebuilding my life, and it helped to take my mind off the pain and the extreme difficulty I had in putting one foot in front of the other. My confused thoughts had little or no continuity but, somehow, they were on the right wavelength.

At last I reached the hut and greatly relieved to get there. The journey had drained the last ounces of strength from my body and I collapsed on the floor and slept instantly. A heavy goods train, trundling past my hut, brought me back to consciousness. It was dark now and the end of the most terrible Sunday of my life. My thoughts were now centred around survival and I thanked God that the goods trains had not been running at the time I was lying on the line.

I struggled to my feet in time to see the last of the wagons disappear from sight and rumble on into the darkness. Despite my exhausted condition, I felt the need to get away from the fetid atmosphere within the hut but, as my legs went from under me, I realised that I needed as much rest as I could get to prepare myself for the long trek in the morning.

In the darkness I thought about the gigantic task that lay ahead. The address of the Samaritans was sixteen miles away. I lay still and sweated into my already filthy clothes. There was nothing to change into and nowhere to wash my body. Thrusting aside thoughts of how people might react to my appearance, I concentrated on how I was going to travel all that way to the Samaritans. The possibility of getting a lift was remote. I was sure that no one in their right mind would stop for me, so instead I tried to concentrate on resting and conserving what little strength I had left.

Having slept fitfully, I decided to begin the journey at day-break. The odds against meeting anyone I knew, so early in the morning, were in my favour. I eased my aching body out of the hut to greet the first rays of sunlight and struggled down the embankment on to a road that I had driven along hundreds of times. But today, walking, it seemed a different road and very long. As the sun rose higher in the sky the intermittent traffic built up into the early morning rush-hour. I walked and rested... walked and rested...

Off to my left I saw a small village. My body was screaming for a drink, I had to go and ask for some water. As I approached the houses they appeared deserted so it was a relief that, further on, I saw a man working in a small garage. I had a forlorn hope that he might offer a cup of tea but he gave me a cup of water and I was duly grateful. On returning to the main road I decided, as a last resort, to try my luck at hitching.

The very first car I thumbed stopped and I was elated as I settled into a comfortable seat. I tried to conceal the way I looked and told the driver the same story I had told the man who had given me a drink... 'my car had broken down and I was stranded...' It seemed futile and I do not suppose either of them believed me but I felt more at ease with the lie – the truth was too fantastic.

Finding the Samaritans was easy and I can never fully express my gratitude for the wonderful way they welcomed me. It was as though my whole being had held itself together just so that I could arrive at their office. Due to the events that followed my memories are vague. My first major recollection was of a visit to the Social Services department and then a visit to a psychiatric hospital. To some people a psychiatric hospital still conjures up visions of mad men and women raving uncontrollably. For me it indicated the possibility of a new life.

On my arrival, I was taken to an office and after a short wait two lady doctors (whom I later discovered were also psychiatrists) asked me questions. 'What day? What month? What year?' My answers were so extreme that the serious expression on their faces was sobering. It was then that I was properly admitted and given a bath under the supervision of two male nurses. Finally, I was put to bed in a small room of my own with a hot drink and four enormous tablets that took away the withdrawal symptoms in seconds. It was the first deep, contented sleep that I had experienced for over five years. The tablets were partly responsible but, in my heart, I knew that I was at peace with myself for the first time since Janeen had left me in that car park a hundred years ago.

Life in a mental hospital was completely different to anything I had ever imagined. My sleep lasted right through the day, and the night was only interrupted by the visit of a male nurse with another four tablets, each the size of a blow-football. The following morning I was allowed to sleep on through breakfast and did not join the rest of the patients until lunchtime. There were about twenty men with ages ranging from eighteen to eighty. The older ones were unable to talk properly or feed themselves, while, at the other end of the scale, there were about ten patients who were either just out of school or had been studying for their 'A' levels. These young men were all suffering from various forms of nervous breakdown. I was soon made aware that the largest 'middle-group' had all been very successful in their chosen careers. We represented a wide cross-section of the public that included an optician, a publican, an electrical contractor, a factory manager and a turf accountant. Their breakdowns had been caused by overwork or excessive worry, but there were others, like myself, with self-inflicted mental wounds caused by our addiction to drink or drugs.

Very few psychiatric hospitals, as I was to discover, had separate alcoholic units and this one was no exception. Alcoholics were very often the odd ones out but I was not really bothered. Because alcoholics suffer from a disease for which there is no known cure, we were not included when the others went for their treatments each morning. We did not, envy them in any way because one of the treatments was E CT (Electro convulsive therapy). I have seen a screaming schizophrenic completely cured by this treatment, but I have also seen some patients turned into frightened, withdrawn, and generally pathetic human wrecks. These images are vividly imprinted on my mind.

Throw any group of people together and there are bound to be some 'characters' who will create humorous situations. In this hospital we shared many hilarious moments, although some were very dramatic at the time and only humorous in retrospect. There was Stefan, whose bed was in the open ward opposite the individual bedrooms. It was the first evening that I had been allowed to sit up with other patients when Frank, an old inmate, folded his paper and, looking at his watch, said, ''Bout time Stefan bailed out George.'

As if in answer, a frantic voice shouted, 'My plane ees un fire, am beeling out. My plane ees un fire, am beeling out.' Then there was the sound of glass smashing and a scream as male nurses grabbed the would-be parachutist before he disappeared through the third-floor window. It later transpired that Stefan had been a distinguished fighter pilot with the Free Polish Air Force in the Second World War.

Middle-aged Oscar was always bragging about his sexual conquests and the incredible number of women he could satisfy at any one time. When stories of Oscar's exploits reached the women's wards, Polly (a lady who was about the same age as Oscar and sexually frustrated) decided to pay him a visit. Somehow, she managed to find his room and conceal herself until 'lights out'. Shortly afterwards pandemonium broke out and everyone was up and awake. The outcome was a very pale Oscar, an extremely disappointed Polly and a delighted psychiatrist. Oscar was later released – as completely cured! There had not been a single 'conquest' story from Oscar following Polly's visit.

But there were some very sad cases where it was difficult to imagine the patient ever being cured. One woman, in her early forties, had lost two children in a car accident ten years previously. She would walk around the grounds holding their imaginary hands and taking them for a walk. Then suddenly, as if returning to reality, she would throw herself to the ground, sobbing uncontrollably.

A young man of twenty was convinced he was an 'alien being' from another planet. He could describe the 'other world' so colourfully it was difficult at times not to believe that it really did exist.

Several young men were 'suicidal' and a few 'tried' while I was there.

The male nurses had an unenviable job but were marvellous in every way. I have since read about many cases of bad treatment being inflicted by members of the mental nursing profession, but in this hospital their behaviour was exemplary.

I was interviewed many times by a lady psychiatrist but I felt that my disease (the medical profession had only recently regarded alcoholism as a disease) was still something of a mystery to her. She spoke to me in terms of learning to control my craving for a drink. One might as well ask a drug addict not to use much heroin! The only cure for any sort of addiction is complete abstinence. There are tablets which are marvellous in combating withdrawal symptoms, and there is a treatment to build up the alcoholic after long periods without food. But when the hospitals have given the patient back his strength and 'dried him out' the rest is up to the alcoholic.

I was unable to tell the doctors how long I had gone without food, but I admitted not having had regular meals for over six months. On admission I weighed eight stone, but my correct weight was nearer eleven. I had lost three stone through lack of food and, as I had always been lightly built, the weight loss was considerable. So in addition to the four large tablets every four hours (plus tablets I could not identify), I was given a vitamin injection every morning for ten days. The thick liquid, which was injected, required a large needle, which was extremely painful, and resulted in heavy bruising and a very sensitive rear end.

I was kept in hospital for over two months and made close friends with many of the patients. One of them was a publican, and he offered me a barman's job and a home to go with it after my discharge. The absurdity of taking up such an offer was painfully obvious. Brian meant well and, right up to the last minute, I was undecided, because I had been offered another job, as a caretaker in a house that had been divided into ten bedsits. It would be a safe job, but totally boring, so I finally decided to go with Brian. I anticipated a very good working relationship and it was agreed that I would start on the Saturday after my Friday discharge.

On the day I left hospital I felt very emotional and, as I thanked the staff, I remember lingering on for far longer than was necessary. From the wreck of a human being lying on a railway line, via the Samaritans, the staff of the hospital had restored my sobriety, sanity and peace of mind. I walked away from the massive building carrying my few possessions in a small plastic bag. Two months had been my longest stay in any one place for over two years, and I was suddenly conscious of how secure I had been behind those solid walls. Taking a firm grip on my bag, I inhaled deeply and headed across the hospital courtyard and up the driveway to the main road.

The driveway was long, with trees, bushes and flowerbeds lining either side. A summer breeze on my hands and face was as a warm caress, and perfume from the flowers filled my nostrils with a gentle fragrance. In the distance I heard the rumble of heavy traffic and, as I drew closer to the main road, it magnified into a hideous roar. I felt an inexplicable panic and broke out in a cold sweat. I was riveted to the spot and shaking like a frightened puppy on seeing traffic for the first time. For several minutes I was quite unable to move then, to my relief, a nurse on a bicycle pulled up alongside and helped me to a nearby bench. I was now shaking uncontrollably and my shirt was soaked in sweat. After a few minutes I began to feel slightly better, and the nurse reminded me that adjusting to the outside world would be difficult. After ten minutes I assured her I would be all right and she wished me well and rode off.

I waited almost an hour for the bus and arrived at my destination feeling as bad as ever. I had previously made up my mind to follow the advice of Alcoholics Anonymous and finish with drinking completely, and now my resolution faced its toughest test when I alighted from the bus right opposite a pub.

My sudden return to the outside world had left me shattered – I had to have a drink. I was still shaking as I drink a double brandy and downed four more before setting off to find Brian.

10

Bits and Pieces

The week that followed was dreadful in every way. I was drinking more than ever before and, inevitably, Brian asked me to leave. He was sorry for me but what good was sympathy? That night I slept in a churchyard. Brian had given me a week's wages and I had filled my pockets with miniature brandies that I had found stored in the bedroom. The next day I searched for a better shelter, but there was nowhere that I could doss down and remain hidden.

In true 'dosser' tradition I refused to spend any money on accommodation, every penny had to be kept for drink and the churchyard to which I returned was free. Finding a very old tombstone that sheltered at least half my body from the elements, I soon fell asleep although, later, the cold night air kept waking me and from then on I dozed fitfully. Suddenly I was fully awake, and this time I could feel in my bones that what had woken me was not just the cold. I looked around and saw the beam from a torch and a dark shadowy figure walking, furtively, in my direction. There was something about the way the figure moved that was far from ordinary and who in his right mind would want to walk through a churchyard in the dead of night anyway? The figure came closer and, unless it changed direction, would pass me on either side of my hiding place. Silently I pulled out another miniature brandy and swallowed the contents. At that moment I lost sight of the shadowy figure and raised myself slowly upwards. As my eyes cleared the top of the tombstone I saw a helmet that could only belong to a policeman. At that precise second my stomach took offence to the last brandy and a large bubble of gas raced to the surface. In the silent churchyard it was the loudest belch ever heard and the policeman's head whipped round. With my usually white face whitened by the torch-beam and seemingly disembodied – I heard an explosively whispered 'Christ!' The torch fell to the ground and the policeman turned and ran. My immediate concern was to find alternative sleeping arrangements in case the officer returned with reinforcements.

I had a feeling that it was going to be 'one of those nights' and I was not to be disappointed. The more I walked the more desperate became my need for somewhere to lie down. Deep within the soul of the homeless alcoholic vagrant is a feeling of utter hopelessness. This is particularly true if he is constantly trying to fight the addiction, yet believes that alcohol is only one of many problems, rather than the one fundamental flaw creating all his imperfections. How pleasant to enjoy a long walk and arrive home and settle into a comfortable chair... For the vagrant there is no end to his walk, only stopping places along the way.

The caravan was parked on a piece of land that had quite recently been cleared by a demolition company, to judge from the amount of machinery lying around. It was an ordinary caravan, obviously old, and used by the workmen for tea and lunch-breaks. For me it was as good as the London Hilton. There was a padlock on the door but I soon prised it open. The interior was in total darkness except when the headlights of a passing car illuminated the confined space. Feeling my way around, my fingers located a small gas stove. Fumbling along a nearby shelf I found a box of matches. What a stroke of luck! I lit the small stove and the glow led me to discover tea, sugar and a small tin of evaporated milk. My luck had certainly changed for the better. After brewing a mug of tea I poured in the contents of two miniature brandies, then sat down on one of the narrow bench seats and savoured the temporary luxury. Further investigation produced a battered alarm clock and an old blanket. After testing its ability to ring I set the alarm for six a.m., then draped the blanket round me and went to sleep.

By noon the following day, after a brief night's sleep, I had walked two or three miles in bright sunshine. The alarm clock had gone off all right and I was, therefore, well away before any of the workmen arrived. On leaving the caravan I had decided to play a hunch. It was a long shot but without anywhere else to go, it was worth a try.

I had never cancelled my acceptance of the caretaker job and the lady, to whom I had spoken on the telephone, had seemed very friendly and understanding. It occurred to me that I would be exactly a week late. It would be easy, therefore, to make up a story about a misunderstanding over the dates and remind her that I had said I would have to visit my parents last week... It worked like a charm. Although puzzled that she could have made such a silly mistake, I was made very welcome.

From the moment I closed the door of my new bedsit I again vowed to stop drinking. My supply of miniature brandies was exhausted. At this point my blood-alcohol level was still high enough to avoid suffering from withdrawal, and it is always easier to make vows of abstinence when there is no craving. Many times I have observed friends and relations stating their intention of giving up smoking while inhaling deeply on a cigarette. But by early evening I had started the withdrawal symptoms.

It was a familiar pattern and very frightening. I had to be alone, completely and utterly alone. Just a bed in a quiet room, a jug of water and complete silence. For vagrant sufferers their private bedroom is the hedgerow or some abandoned building, without water or food, and only the bone-penetrating cold for company. Tonight I was lucky. I tried to control the shakes by hugging my body and restlessly pacing up and down. Later I started to sweat. Pain like a gentle toothache crept around deep inside my guts and grew in area and intensity until I was writhing in agony. I had to strip off the few clothes I had been wearing because of the sweating and the fact that, as part of the withdrawal pains, my skin was extremely itchy and sensitive. By now my whole body was oiled in an evil-smelling slime and any sudden noise – a car backfiring or a door slamming – would make me jump.

The mental states of fear, shame and rage upstaged each other in my fevered brain as well as remorse for the horrible waste of friendships, talent and money. I cursed alcohol... I hated it and everything about it and, between the crescendos of pain, I moaned the filthiest obscenities at anything and anybody that sprang to mind for making me suffer. The real obscenity was that one decent drink could end my suffering, but desperately I was fighting back. From previous experience I knew that part of the agony was psychological... just knowing that there was no alcohol in the room, no instant cure if I couldn't hold out. But somehow the hours passed and the pain gradually eased. I could now lie reasonably still on my bed, but I was fevered, exhausted and unable to sleep. With an intense effort of will I eventually struggled out of bed and made myself half-way presentable. My duties as caretaker only required about an hour's work morning and evening – payment was the free accommodation. As soon as I had finished my duties I shuffled back to my room and collapsed. I had used up every last ounce of strength.

It was late in the evening before the pain resolved itself into a dull ache, and I still hadn't slept. I almost forgot the evening's chores but just managed to force myself out on my rounds. By the next morning I was able to face a cup of tea and, by the end of the third day, I spread some butter on a slice of bread. Drinking tea had been agony as my throat had closed up, and now I spent the best part of an hour getting the bread into my stomach. Even that simple exercise caused me to sweat and shake, but, by the end, I fell into my first peaceful sleep since the withdrawal had started. The next day I managed a small meal. I was emerging from the tunnel. On the fifth day, after another good night's sleep, I was fit enough to face up to the idea of full-time work and drink! DRINK!? That was the alcoholic's schizophrenia coming into play with a vengeance – the inability to distinguish reality from delusion. I believed I could now drink normally if I chose – no problem! – and began to make plans for the future. Nevertheless, for the present, I abstained.

I had to entertain again, to get in front of an audience and earn my living in the only way I knew; but first I would have to get a job. My landlady had given me the names of various factories on a nearby industrial estate and I immediately began my search for a job. It was a beautiful town surrounded by a range of magnificent hills, and that summer was one of the finest I could remember.

I had met up with Martin, someone else I had made friends with in the hospital. He lived about a mile away, and as he had a car we regularly went out together. Despite some strenuous efforts I was unable to find a job of any sort. Had it not been for Martin, his sister Sue, and Alan, her husband, I think I would have lost my reason altogether.

Weeks on the dole turned into months. The local music shop was a magnet and I soon made friends with the young manager named Michael. It turned out that he also was a musician and keen to start up a group. We had a lot in common. The fact that all the instruments and amplifiers could be hire-purchased through Michael's firm made things very easy. So a group was quickly formed and the first rehearsal arranged for a Monday evening in a room over the shop.

I was as excited as a child on its way to its first party and feeling very confident and optimistic about the future. It was now five months since my return and the night of severe withdrawal. Since then no alcohol had passed my lips.

All the equipment was laid out waiting. It represented a big commitment. The lads arrived and the rehearsal got underway with only my personal demon waiting in the wings for, half-way through, I experienced an insatiable urge for alcohol and could not wait to get out of the enclosed space. The rehearsal was brought to a premature end as I made an excuse about feeling faint and needing some fresh air.

I decided to try to walk the urge out of my system. After an hour I felt no better and was perspiring freely. Finally I could stand it no longer and entered a pub. I ordered a pint of beer, then another and another, convinced that my long lay-off had cured my addiction and that I could now drink socially like normal people.

Within a week I was back on the hard stuff and wrapped in a cocoon of fantasy shot through with delusions of grandeur. Walter Mitty wasn't in the same league. For short periods between the fantasies, I realised that alcohol made me schizophrenic and, for equally short periods, that knowledge scared the hell out of me.

Two weeks passed and I now owed money to many people, including Martin's sister and her husband. As my drinking was again affecting other people's lives I would have to get away, and I made up my mind to go back to London. I felt a great deal of remorse for the way I had treated Sue and Alan, especially as they had a young family to support. To borrow from them when I knew I would be unable to pay them back typified how low I was prepared to sink. Having drunk all the money I had borrowed, I had to wait until Saturday morning for my cheque from the Social Security. Time passed slowly and I lay low to avoid my many creditors.

Saturday finally arrived and, having collected my money, I was just setting out to walk to the station when Sue and Alan arrived. They said how much they had missed me and that I was not to worry about the money I owed them. I felt awful but my mind was made up. They even took me to the railway station and I promised faithfully to write and repay my debt. The train left punctually and headed south – to another nightmare.

11

Michelle Explains

The train sped along, eating up the miles with a contempt that would have silenced the most cynical of British Rail detractors. As I relaxed in the comfortable warmth of the carriage, my head was full of thoughts of the city and whatever destiny held in store for me.

During the day I had enormous quantities of drink and my memory of subsequent events is very hazy. There was a girl, foreign... but I cannot be more specific. The first inkling I had that it was morning again was on seeing small square pebble-glass windows that filtered the sunlight, and the terrible throbbing in my head. I felt sick, and for a moment thought I was back in hospital, but I was not to be that lucky.

Lifting my head to look around, a searing pain shot across my cheek then up into the temple area and back again. Instinctively my hand went up to touch the source of the pain and that hurt too. What the hell...? I grumbled, bewildered, and forced my body into a sitting position. It took a lot of physical effort to get there, but very little mental effort to come to the conclusion that I had been in a fight. There was dried blood all over my hands and I just knew my face was the same. My whole body was tender beyond words.

I looked around and thought that I must be in a police cell when the rattle of a key in the lock and the appearance of a uniformed constable confirmed it.

'Out!'

The one word rang through the cell and I foolishly thought about how good the acoustics were, but this fellow did not want a concert – only to be obeyed. With a struggle I got to my feet and stumbled out into a warm passageway and was then guided by a heavy hand towards a door.

'You've got three minutes to make yourself presentable, lad. You're not a pretty sight and no mistake.'

I was grateful for the warm water and soap but it was a painful ablution. Then I was taken to the busy outer office and the desk sergeant.

'Give Dr Kissinger his belongings back, Jim,' quipped the senior man, and an envelope was produced and tipped out on to the counter in front of me.

'Check it, Mr Charles, and any more tricks like you tried to pull last night and you'll be charged.'

The caution stung like hell and my curiosity was aroused, despite the usual remorse I felt for anything I might have done. They had not locked me up without cause but I could not remember a damn thing after arriving in the West End.

'Look, officer, I'm very sorry for whatever inconvenience I have caused, but I met some old friends I had not seen for years and I honestly cannot recall a thing. What did I get arrested for?' The sergeant looked surprised for a moment and then his expression changed.

'Yes, I suppose you were in a bit of a state. Well, you were with two French girls at the Savoy hotel trying to book in as Dr Kissinger's 'aide-de-camp'. Your American accent was pretty good and your joint descriptions fitted a trio who have been conning hotels throughout London. The hotel manager called us in and you came quietly at first but then you tried to get away. It took two of our officers to get you into the car.'

I fingered a few bruises and knew what he meant. He pushed the contents of the envelope towards me and I began to look through them. I counted fifty-eight pounds, plus nearly three pounds in change, a few cigarette coupons and a phone number written on a dirty piece of paper.

The money was an absolute mystery and I sat outside the police station on a bench in complete bewilderment. The more I thought about the previous night the less I could remember; the only consolation was the mystery money I now had in my pocket.

I started walking towards Piccadilly Circus and stopped at the first café that offered breakfast. Despite the lousy hangover and the foul taste in my mouth I was ravenous, and ordered double bacon and egg from a young Italian waiter. It was difficult trying to swallow because the throat and stomach contract after excessive drinking and no food. I managed to fight down the pain of swallowing, finished the whole meal and sat back with a cup of coffee and took stock. The café was on the small side but extremely clean and tidy. Reaching into my pocket I drew out the envelope containing my belongings. I counted the money slowly and was putting it away carefully when I spotted the grubby piece of paper bearing the phone number. I still did not recognise it, and for the umpteenth time mulled over the night before... Dr Kissinger's aide-de-camp? Great!

I paid my bill and went out into the busy street with the intention of finding a telephone box. Locating a box was one thing, to find one in working order proved a little more difficult, and then I had to wait in a queue. The number rang out for a long time and I was about to give up when a female voice answered.

'Oh, good m-morning,' I stammered. 'I hope you'll forgive me for ringing, but I have had an accident and it has caused partial amnesia. I found your telephone number on a piece of paper and it occurred to me that you might be able to throw a little light on what happened to me yesterday?'

'Is your name Neek?'

My confidence wavered. 'Yes Yes, I'm Nick. Did we meet yesterday?'

'You really do not remember? Well, you must have been veree drunk.' The accent was French and I thought how attractive it sounded.

'Look, I don't even know your name, but could we meet?' I think I must have sounded desperate.

'Of course! Where are you now?'

I told her and she said to go to the corner of George Street and Gloucester Place where she would be waiting.

I hailed a cab and arrived to find many passers-by but no one waiting. Ten minutes later I was about to ring again when I saw a young woman running in my direction. She was about twenty-four, blonde, quite attractive and dressed in a sloppy sweater and jeans.

'Sorry to have kept you waiting – have you been here long?'

The accent was very slight, just a faint slurring. I suggested a drink, telling her that after last night what made me bad might just make me better.

'Ah! You English have some funny ways but I know a place. Come on...'

I waited until we had settled down with a drink before asking her name.

'Can you remember nothing of last night at all?'

I shook my head in reply.

'Well I can fill some of it in for you. You were with another French girl in the Savoy foyer and, by coincidence, we share the same Christian name – Michelle – very common in our country. You were demanding in a loud voice a room for you and your wife and were refusing to pay in advance. I think you said you were in politics or something and you had a terrible American accent. They had just called the police when one of the hotel security men caught me soliciting.'

My eyes turned quickly away from the cigarette I was lighting and looked her full in the face.

'...Yes, I am a prostitute, but of course I denied it – saying I was with you. You see, the other Michelle, the girl you were with, is also a prostitute and we are friends. It was a "long shot" as the Americans say, but at the time I thought you might cover for me.'

Her eyes glinted wickedly when she used the American slang and I realised she was enjoying herself.

'Just then the police arrived and they took the three of us away in their car, although you struggled and they had to manhandle you a little. When we arrived at the police station we were left alone in a corridor and I stuffed my money in your pocket in case the police confiscated it, as I have a record. You agreed to say that you had dated both of us and would take us for drinks in your room at the hotel, and you kept your word. The police kept you for the night, but we were allowed home... That's about it.'

I said nothing for a while, as I realised rather ruefully that phoning the mystery number was about to cost me all my mystery money.

'Bit of a coincidence meeting your friend, wasn't it?'

'Not really.' Michelle took a sip of her drink and I thought that she really was intelligent and attractive, not at all what I had imagined. 'We only cover the hotels in and around Piccadilly and meet quite often.' She looked at me with an amused expression and I got the distinct impression she was taking more than just a passing interest in me. It seemed like a good idea at the time to put my 'con' ability to the test, although I had a suspicion that I was not in the same league as Michelle.

'Well, I suppose I had better return your money. The trouble is I don't know which is yours and which is mine. After paying you, the remainder will be all I have in the world.' I lowered my eyes and pulled the money from my back pocket. Silence. Then Michelle let out the most raucous female laugh I had ever heard.

'Look, if you want the money you can have it. I've got plenty and I don't have to answer to anyone.' She continued laughing and I felt myself shrinking ... all the early morning tipplers were looking in our direction.

'Okay! Thanks! It was a bit pointless trying my act out on you but I would like to keep the money and I'll pay it back as soon as I get set-up and—'

'There you go again,' she interrupted. 'Why do you say you will pay me back when you know and I know that you will not ...eh?'

This French girl was way ahead of me and I had the feeling that, yet again, life was going to be very tough in London.

'I'm sorry if I made you feel small but you must think of the money as a gift... okay?'

It was the first time I had lost a verbal battle of wits with anyone – far less a woman.

Her voice and expression mellowed as she asked, 'When did you arrive in London, Neek?'

I told her, and suddenly the complete truth was spilling out. When I had finished Michelle took a deep breath.

'Phew! and I thought I had problems. I've met a lot of junkies in London and I suppose it's a similar sort of thing. Do you think you will ever beat it?'

'I guess I'll find a way, but sometimes I really despair.' I felt her hand inside mine. 'Could you possibly put me up for a couple of nights... ? I won't be a nuisance I promise you.'

Her expression changed and she shook her head.

'I'm sorry, Neek, I can't. I only have a bedsit and I'm watched like a hawk. They know I am a call-girl and, given the slightest excuse, I would be out. That's why I work the hotels because I can't take anyone back home.'

I was sorry I had asked and changed the subject. 'Shall we have another drink?'

'No thanks, I must go; but give me a ring if you want to. Good luck!' She kissed my cheek and was gone.

I sat for a long time feeling very alone in the world, then headed for Piccadilly.

12

A Bridge Too Far

The London traffic noise and the shape of the man next to me materialised simultaneously; he was trying to rub circulation into his toes. It seemed silly to take off your shoes and socks when it was so cold and I shook myself to see if I really had regained consciousness or whether I was dreaming. He rubbed the little toe too hard because it fell off and he tossed it at me playfully. I threw up, but not because the frozen toe hit my lips, it was the hair lacquer containing alcohol that we had drunk the night before. It contained something that solidified in your stomach and when you were sick it tore chunks out of your throat on the way out. I looked at the toe and pushed it with my foot.

'I won't have to wash that one again!'

Fred was a hard bastard, I once saw him stab the broken neck of a bottle into a sleeping drunk to see if he could wake him up. He was smiling a sickly smile.

'Did you hear?'

'Yes,' I said.

He replaced a filthy sock and rotted shoe and ambled off.

'Harry Hat's going!'

The voice belonged to someone behind me and I had to turn around to see the speaker. As I did so I saw Harry walking towards the river which was about half a mile away. I had known him for about a year and I never once saw him without the hat; it was said he even wore it to sleep on the rare occasions he stayed at the Sally Army. I followed him at a distance, intrigued. There was something final about the words that had been spoken, but I wanted to know where Harry was going, after all he owed me a fag. He got to London Bridge and turned down the steps which led to the river. When I got there all that was left was the hat just floating on its own. Harry had had enough.

'See what I mean?'

The voice was behind me again.

'Somebody's got to do something!' I said.

'Nobody cares!' said the voice.

'I bloody care!' I cried.

'And what the hell can you do?'

'I'll bloody well do something, I swear I will!'

'Bollocks!' said the voice.

I looked back towards the hat which was rapidly disappearing into the distance. For just a moment I thought I saw Harry's hand come up from out of the depths in an effort to take it with him to heaven, or hell, but it was a trick of the light or the meths. I stumbled back up the steps to other people's civilisation, my head swimming, and wondered inanely if Harry had swum a stroke or two before death – a sheet of blue, grey and finally blackness.

13

The Night I Bought my Life
for a Pound

No clean hospital ward this time, just a heap of rotting cardboard and evil-smelling food waste. I moved my head towards the sky and ached in silence.

Slowly and painfully I struggled towards the end of the world – the Scarborough Street Social Security office for the homeless. I pushed my way through the turnstile gate entrance, and fell to the floor on top of someone else's mess and waited.

The doctor took my pulse – I do not know where he came from, who called him or why. He gave me tablets, Librium I think, and a glass of water with which to swallow them. I felt better almost at once. He led me outside and wrote an address on the back of a business card.

'Go here and tell them I sent you,' was all he said.

The address was at the Aldgate end of Middlesex Street in London's East End. It was a place of generous charitable aid for life's casualties run by one John Profumo, a former Minister for War in the Government, best remembered for something best forgotten, given his atonement.

I received a bath and some clean clothes and we talked of Valerie Hobson (Profumo's Hollywood actress wife) and the theatres, clubs and pubs I had worked. I was relieved of a prescription the doctor had given me hidden in an envelope.

The tablets worked a miracle. I spent the day in and out of a fitful sleep.

At around four p.m. a social worker arrived and gave me an East End hostel address, the cab fare and everyone wished me well.

I had stayed in all sorts of hostels, some were better than others, but this place was the most frightening, as well as the most depressing. It seemed predominantly a halfway-house for former prisoners on parole awaiting job interviews, or alternatively those on bail awaiting trial. The remainder can be best described as thoroughly evil men who would slit a throat for the price of a drink or less, and in fact did just that.

I was tipped off by the foreman that I should sleep in my clothes and to stuff my shoes into my pillow-case if I still wanted them in the morning. Although this did nothing for my peace of mind, it was the fear of the physical harm that kept me awake most of my first night. The second was not much better, but the third night the man in the next bed lost his life and I bought mine for a pound.

I could feel the tension in the air. I can smell trouble even to this day, and this night reeked of war and I was in the middle of it. A man had been recognised at the breakfast table as the 'grass' from a court case long ago by the man whom he had shopped, and the hate was as thick as the morning porridge.

I turned in early, to get out of the way as much as anything else, but began to regret it almost at once. I could hear a lot of heated chatter and some words I could just distinguish floated my way from time to time.

'His bed is next to the new bloke they call Brummie Nick.'

'What time does he get in?'

I pondered for a moment on whether to spend a night out, but decided it would give a guilty impression and stayed put, drawing the bedclothes high over my head.

I must have gone to sleep because suddenly I was acutely aware of the darkness which follows lights out, and the accompanying silence... Then I could hear stealthy footsteps and stifled conversation.

I moved my head slowly to my left and could vaguely make out the sleeping form of the man in the next bed and was conscious of his gentle breathing. Then there were other shapes, a torch flashed briefly on, then off, and there was a thud, a sickening thud followed by a muffled grunt then the sound of water running. It soaked me, I could feel it all over. It blinded me as I opened my eyes and I struggled to my feet just as the room was flooded with light. At once I saw two men by the next bed, wild-eyed and as surprised to see me as I was them, but it was the bed itself that held my attention. The occupant was dead, that was obvious; a gaping wound stretched east to west beneath his chin and the red liquid pumped like water. I had seen from an underground stream. The man who had reason to hate held the knife, which dripped blood not water. I snapped from my frozen state just as the two intruders did the same and they moved menacingly towards the only witness to their horrendous crime. I could actually smell the alcohol on the nearest man's breath when I heard myself speak.

'Look! I didn't see a thing, I'll go now and you'll never see me again.'

I brushed my hand across my face and it was then that I saw the blood – all over my hands and down my front. I was covered. I realised the force of the dead man's blood had sprayed me like a hose. I had heard stories of the force of blood when the jugular vein was severed; this was the proof.

I was now petrified as the reality of my position registered and I heard myself begging for my life, then I had a brainwave. I thrust my hand into my pocket and felt a pound note which represented all I had in the world.

'Here, it's yours, if you let me go.'

The villains seemed to snap out of the murderous mood they were in and the front man took a step back.

'Leave him, he's too scared to grass.' He looked me full in the face and added: 'It took me ten years to find him. You'll spend your life looking over your shoulder if you say one word.'

I threw the note on the bed, the other man snatched it up and they were gone.

What to do, I couldn't think. I was undoubtedly in shock but I had to do something, they might think it was me. There was a bathroom on the same landing as the room I was in and instinctively I picked up my bag and headed for it. I was still fully dressed of course and the blood was now sticky and congealing fast as I removed the shirt and filled the filthy bowl with water. It was stone cold but it could have been a piping hot shower, so grateful was I for its presence. Soon I was clean and free from the scarlet mess, apart from a little which was hardly noticeable around the top of my trousers. I put on my only other shirt and stowed the evidence of the bloody one well away.

Slowly and stealthily I crept down the stairs and went out into the night air and walked and walked and walked. The more I walked the more I thought, and slowly I decided upon a plan.

Nobody knew who I was. I had walked into the hostel off the streets and used, as always, a fictitious name. I had done nothing wrong whatsoever and knew none of those involved, or anything at all about them. I walked to the Salvation Army Hostel in Middlesex Street and heaved a sigh of relief when it was a familiar face on the night staff. He let me in and booked me on at 6 pm, ten hours previously.

'How are you Nick, Where've you been? What you bin doin'?'

'Oh! you know, the usual things,' I muttered. 'Just another day.'

'Goodnight, Nick.'

'Night, George.'

14

Reflections

The following day I obtained special permission from the Salvation Army captain to stay in bed on grounds of ill-health. He had taken one look at my emaciated, shaking body and simply nodded. I lay alone in the enormous dormitory gazing at empty beds stretching almost as far as I could see, and my mind drifted back over the years to my early life.

'You have a lovely voice, Nicholas.'

The school had a rural setting. The teacher had a rural face – round, healthy looking in a way reminiscent of an apple on a tree in any English orchard. It was a strange sensation. I was sort of dreaming but not completely asleep. There were forty other faces around me all aged six plus something, but I cannot recollect the features. Strangely, I do recollect some of the names, Jonathan, Jennifer, Geraldine – Hazel Marlene had a name and a face, she was my first love. We held hands, most days she went to sleep on my shoulder, the teachers didn't seem to mind, there was no reason why they should – they were days of innocence, sunshine and sweet-smelling flowers.

As is often the way, we do not appreciate the beautiful things as they happen, it is not until later that the full beauty becomes obvious and we wish we had recognised it at the time. Then we could have breathed its beauty, smelled its fragrance and enjoyed the fact that it was just happening.

It must have been Christmas time because I stood in front of morning assembly and sang 'Away in a Manger' in front of six hundred fellow scholars. Some sniggered, some looked appreciative, a few looked bewildered, Hazel looked enchanted so I sang to her.

I did not know it at the time, how could I, but I had just had my first audience reaction, good, bad and indifferent. There was no way of knowing either, that I had taken my first faltering step along years of a bad road.

It had all started well enough of course. Church choir at seven years of age, my first rock 'n' roll group at thirteen, fronting my first decent-sized big band before I left school and signing my first record contract before my seventeenth birthday. Sadly, though unaware, I had begun a fifteen-year apprenticeship as an alcoholic. I had recorded many tracks, some good, some bad, some indifferent. Most are lost to me, although I have no doubt some survive in dusty corners of other people's lives. Everyone talks about the sixties being an exciting time. I suppose they were, but for me the revolution in music and fashion was the mid to late fifties. The big bands were a fading memory, teddy boys in drainpipe trousers, luminous socks, gaudy shirts, pencil-thin ties and velvet-flashed, long jackets hit the streets and particularly the dance halls. Cinemas were utilising their stage areas for the new rock bands and the first ten rows of seats were removed to allow an area for dancing – cinemas were definitely on the way out.

I am sure every town and village had its slick Brylcreemed pacesetters – my home town in Worcestershire had been magnificently represented by Peter Elliot. He was handsome in a Mediterranean sort of way, and was able to follow the fashion more easily than most because his father was a well-off local shopkeeper. My two outstanding memories of Peter were of him walking past my house in full regalia with not a hair out of place, and of him covered in sores, standing next to me washing up in a city restaurant, one week before he was murdered in a knife fight.

For me, my private roller-coaster decline ran on its own self-built track oblivious of bureaucracy, any house rules and most definitely anyone's feelings. I created my own mayhem. It began with each first mouthful which was as wonderful in the moment, as the memory of Hazel was in the past. Spencer Tracy changed in ninety seconds of cinematographic genius from handsome, successful Dr Jekyll into hairy, ugly, shameful Mr Hyde. Alcohol, from my standpoint, made me more self-assured, a better driver, a better singer, more handsome, more popular, more successful – I was misinformed. From the point of view of others, particularly my little sister Judy who adored me throughout our childhood, I became insufferably cocky, drove irresponsibly and sang out of tune for the first time in my life. I lost my visual appeal, became hopelessly boring, lost my ability to achieve and with it my credibility and self-esteem.

In my middle age I would meet one of my former schoolteachers who would tell me that I had had as a youngster the potential to become a first-class goalkeeper. It was not until he did so that I recalled that I did have a gift in that direction; predictably, I refused the position in our school team, preferring to be a goalscorer instead, an ambition I did not have the ability to achieve.

I do remember being a top company salesman. I do recall writing advertising slogans for commercial television. I can never forget bandleader/songwriter Billy Reid telling me in my twenties that in his view I had as much talent at the same age as Frank Sinatra. I believed him. 'He should know,' I told listeners in some bar or another, 'he wrote one of Sinatra's biggest hits.'

I did not tell them how he cried when he found me in a pool of my own urine on Euston Station some years later, and walked away from me for ever.

I came back to the present and decided insanely that the best way to deal with the physical and emotional pain was the hair of the dog – or perhaps several hairs. I struggled slowly down the concrete stairs and pushed past a startled doorman into the street.

Time and space became infinite.

Pews? Church? Abbey? Peace! Cathedral! Perhaps...

My eyes came back into focus – pain came back to relevance. Vomit over the staff of a sidesman's cross. I wiped away the disgusting liquid on expensive drapes.

A collection plate came into focus before me, left there irresponsibly by a careless cleric or veritable verger.... My hand stretched out before me determined by the devil.

'I do hope you're not gonna take money from that tray, young man.'

The voice belonged to the loudest female American tourist in the world.

I have often been asked 'What was my rock bottom?' I could have told of waking to find rats gnawing at my torso – possibly waking in a public place soaked in my own urine and excrement – court appearances, the inevitable shame.

I think none of these. I pulled my hand back from the collection plate and slunk away from the American woman and her accusation, suffering the greatest humiliation of all.

My legs would not carry me far. I sat in the nearest pew and looked up at the massive stained-glass window before me. The sun dazzled, dulled only slightly by the blues, reds, greens and yellows. I looked down deep into my lap so as to avoid the accusing stares of those who might have witnessed my shame. I became aware of shafts of coloured light – there were two, both red, one on my left arm, the other on my right, I felt the warmth but not the message. Jesus phoned for help. My eyes opened then closed in time with the momentum of the flashing blue light and blood ran down my front.

'He's bleeding from the ears!' said a voice. The pain in my stomach felt like a knife wound.

'Slow the bloody ambulance down or he'll die,' said another. 'He'll die anyway!' replied the first.

I took the blade from my stomach and passed it to the voice.

'I bloody well won't,' I said indignantly sitting upright.

Vaguely I remember seeing the syringe – vaguely I recall feeling the needle – but God only knows how I got the knife.

Pain came with waking. A searing swirling agony that tore at every nerve ending. My mouth was dry and my eyesight blurred, I struggled against nausea and called for help.

Medication arrived and with it some respite, I lay with much to contemplate... again!

It seemed the knife had missed vital organs and needed only a dozen stitches. My face was badly scratched, I know not how – a kindly nurse told me it would heal quickly because I cried constantly – there's salt in tears.

The following week my discharge was delayed because they could not find my clothes. I did not tell them they had been incinerated because they were so dirty, although I felt slight guilt as a search ensued.

Finally, an apology, five pounds from petty cash and three items of clothing from the Social Services lady – canvas beach shoes, no socks, jeans with holes, no undergarment, a T-shirt with poignant stencilled words 'The End is Nigh'. Good job it was a summer's day.

Déjà vu – I had done it all before. Usually the money led to the nearest bar – for some reason today was different. I sat on a newly made ornamental garden wall in a shopping mall gazing into space. Metaphorically, I was as naked as the day I was born. The three items of clothing were not mine, I had nothing to show for thirty years of life, only my mother's unshakeable love.

So much promise. Composer, singer, salesman, husband, father, nothing left. So much wrong in my life. Wives that divorced me, employers who fired me and cars that disintegrated with monotonous regularity. No friends, only those who felt they could benefit if I had the price of a drink. I could not even visit a pub on a Saturday night without getting drunk. So many problems in my life, or perhaps...?

Had drink ruined my marriages? I had lost many a job through drink, perhaps every job I ever had. I was always drunk when the cars became undriveable – and who on earth wants to befriend a drunk apart from perhaps another drunk? And I did not just get drunk on a Saturday night, it was whenever I had enough money, or whenever I drank alcohol. Perhaps it was not that alcohol was a problem in my life but that my problem in life was alcohol. There had been so many pointers along the way, the victim of this disease, however, is always the last to believe.

Elation! I had heard a thousand times in hospitals and meeting rooms the word alcoholic – maybe this was me. It was like a giant penny dropping – like seeing the light. For the first time since my first mouthful I considered the possibility that alcohol was not just one of my problems, but responsible for all of them.

15

Remembrance

The sun was warm on my face and hands and I felt a rare sensation – the warmth penetrating to the very marrow in my bones.

The shoppers milling around distracted me for a moment and I wondered what traumas existed in their lives – what awful skeletons lay in their cupboards? What dreadful secrets did smart suits and fashionable dresses hide?

The people going about their business began to fade into the background, my memory started to flash through scores of tragic lives I had known like the fast-forward on a video. I thought of a time in my life I had spent with Jacob Jones and the awful circumstances in which we met.

I had moved into a condemned building in Hackney with some strange characters in the most primitive conditions imaginable. The cold was intense, there was no electric light or running water except through the roof when it rained, and the existence was miserable. There were four of us, Geoff was an engineer or had been, Gordon a qualified ladies' hairdresser, and Jacob... well! He didn't say much. He was intelligent, that was for sure, because when he did talk you could tell – you could just tell.

We had tried to get him to open up and tell us about himself and his life, but he had always evaded the issue or glossed over the subject. Then, one terribly wet and cold winter's evening as we sat huddled around a six-foot area that was not soaking wet from leaks in the roof, I cornered him.

'Jacob,' I said firmly, 'I'm here because I am a drunk. Geoff is a drunk and Gordon is a compulsive gambler, he would bet on two ants climbing up a wall and once lost a hairdressing salon in a game of cards. What puzzles me is why you are here – you have never let on.'

He looked thoughtful, even sad and there was, in the silence, the promise of an explanation – we said nothing and waited and waited... Suddenly he began. 'It started when my wife left me,' he said. 'I was a manager with a large firm in Surrey working long hours. One night I got home early and caught her in bed with her lover – I was gutted. Prior to this I had not drunk much alcohol. In fact never more than a couple of halves or perhaps two glasses of wine at a session.

'She left the matrimonial home and took the kids with her and it was with total disbelief that I heard she had been granted custody. Well, I went on a bender and got drunk for the very first time in my life and it lasted a month. My first memory of coming through it was becoming conscious after a blackout sitting on a council bench outside a junior school in Hackney. I watched fascinated as the five and six year old girls swung round on the bars and suddenly I realised I was being sexually stimulated by the scene... I was totally horrified. I remember running like a mad thing, and eventually collapsing from sheer exhaustion in a heap on the ground – people came to my aid, I brushed them aside and sobbed in my misery.

'In the months that followed I was able to plot when it had occurred. I had to have at least six pints or the equivalent before my normal sexual preferences gave way to the insane perversion, and so naturally I thought I could control it simply by not drinking so much. It was at this stage that I realised I was hooked. I was an alcoholic – once I had started I simply could not stop. My misery continued, and began to get worse until, during my enforced sober periods due to lack of money, I realised my urges were getting more sinister. It was becoming increasingly likely that my "looking" would turn to "doing", and "doing" would result in going to prison.' He shuffled, then went on. 'One day I gritted my teeth and visited a GP in Stepney and begged for a referral for a hospital detox – he agreed.'

I remember Jacob moving some rubbish on the floor with his foot and looking sheepish, but he took a breath and continued...

'I had a few slips, then one day disaster struck which turned out to be my lucky break. I had been outside an infant girls' school for an hour or so and a member of the public had been alarmed enough to call the police.

'The shock of being arrested was so great that I decided there and then to stop drinking for ever.

'Through all of this I had somehow clung on to my job, mainly due to a long friendship with my boss. I had to confess, however, to working when I could, and he had resorted to paying me hourly and checking almost everything that I did. Inevitably the work meant socialising, and socialising meant alcohol – the job had to go. Quite simply I had tried every combination to survive alcohol-free and the only thing that works for me is living like this.'

There followed the longest silence I can remember and all three of us pondered on Jacob's self-imposed life with horror and amazement. To think this poor wretched creature had to literally live the life of a vagrant, out of respect for humanity, filled us with a humility that would stay imprinted on our minds for the rest of our lives. Whatever crosses we had to bear, none would weigh as heavily as the cross of Jacob Jones.

'Got a light mate?' I snapped back to the present and looked suspiciously at the man before me holding an unlit cigarette. I decided he was an innocent passer-by and struck the match.

The sun had gone behind a cloud and to most folk it would have been slightly chilly – the thought of the Hackney squat made my world feel distinctly warmer. Jacob's life was one of the most awful I'd known, unless of course I included Mavis and David Carter whom I had met in some hospital or another. My God! Thinking of them, brewers and distillers had much to answer for.

Mavis was a district nurse and David an engineer – both in their home village. The small population mostly knew each other and there was a great deal of communal entertainment. The village pubs, of which there were two, were the centre of the local community. Neither Mavis or David were particularly good mixers and it took the annual Christmas pantomime to free them both from their shy, almost timid existence. One evening in autumn there came a knock on the door and the vicar, accompanied by two of the congregation, introduced themselves as the entertainment committee for the village. A meeting followed in the clubroom above the local pub and soon after Mavis and David joined the organising team for the forthcoming yuletide festivity.

Their house was a three-bedroom detached building put together painstakingly with every spare penny they earned, plus a small legacy from David's father's will. They spent the vast majority of their leisure time improving it, but that was about to change. The Christmas pantomime was to be 'Dick Whittington' and it soon emerged that both Mavis and David had hidden talent, and they were cast in the two leading parts. Their entire existence began to revolve around the production, and both were delighted to discover that a couple of glasses of wine each relieved their timidity and gave them all the confidence they needed. Every night saw them rehearsing in the village hall and they took it in turns, with the other cast members, to take along a bottle or two for refreshment. As soon as the rehearsals were over everyone piled down to the pub and a boozy session ended the evening.

They both loved their new-found social lives and continued to surprise each other with the things they did with the extra confidence found from the added glass or two. Mavis, hitherto unable to say boo to a goose, put her supervisor in her place at work, having had a snifter at lunchtime. David was having similar experiences at the factory and joined the set who went to the pub at lunchtime. He felt his presence now dominated the factory and he was becoming a powerful influence.

Some things had changed however. One or two inoffensive folk who had been their friends, did not call any more, though Mavis and David did not worry they found them too boring by far. Mavis had visited one of them, and could not understand why she had not answered the door. She knew she was in as she could see her behind a curtain – it bothered her for only a few minutes and then it passed from her mind. The run-up to the Christmas panto continued.

The big night came, they both thought it a wonderful success and a big party followed; then a hangover to beat all hangovers and then the most awful anticlimax.

Four days after the last night of the panto Mavis suggested that they go to the pub for the evening and it soon became every night – the lunchtime visits continued as well.

During the summer David had a row with a senior manager at work and was sacked for violent conduct. He had only just left the pub from a lunchtime visit and returned there to get over his dismissal. Shortly afterwards, Mavis injected the wrong drug into a patient and was suspended on full pay. Six months later she attended the disciplinary hearing in an intoxicated condition and was sacked on the spot. Two years of boozing night and day followed interrupted only by the birth of a baby they called Susan. Bills began to pile up and a series of jobs for both of them ended in drunken scenarios. One terrible winter's night, the fire brigade awoke the drunken couple and carried them to safety; the baby was dead. The insurance money kept them under the influence for ten months then the mortgage company foreclosed. They were evicted and sat together on the kerb of the road outside and drank a bottle of wine cursing their luck.

One thing will live with Mavis for ever, and to this day I can see the haunted look upon her face as she remembered. 'I was always ashamed to put our empty bottles into the dustbin. The dustbin man lived nearby and I thought neighbours would talk so I stacked them all in the cellar. On the night baby Susan died, we had left her downstairs in the front room with a cigarette burning down the side of the chair. The floor burned through into the cellar, the heat exploded an estimated two thousand bottles, and one hundred and twenty-seven pieces of glass were taken from her tiny body.'

The sun was out again but lower in the sky and the shoppers were getting fewer. I felt sad, not really depressed, just incredulous that shops everywhere were full of products for sale that contained a substance that can kill and change history, maim, deform and cause untold misery yet everyone thinks it okay. To my right was a billboard that showed a scene from the Arizona Desert with a brilliant picture of sun-drenched sand and a huge mountain in the background. In the foreground a handsome cowboy, sweat pouring from his brow... in his hand a pint of ice-cold lager.

I took my five pounds and bought a week's bed-tickets at the Salvation Army.

16

Bombed Out

The following day I met a guy called Jeff in the dining room at the Salvation Army hostel in Middlesex Street during the breakfast session, and he confided to me that his problem was also 'a drinking one'.

Only the night before he had overstayed his welcome at a live-in bar job and had left all his belongings in a battered suitcase, fairly well hidden, in a half-built loo on a building site.

'Nothing worse than lugging a case around when you are looking for a bed,' he had said airily after I had agreed to accompany him on his journey of retrieval, 'but I hope I can find it okay.' We must have walked miles and I was showing extreme disdain at the distance, only slightly comforted by the promise of a swig or two from a bottle of brandy, hidden wrapped in his belongings.

Eventually, and not before time, we rounded a corner and Jeff exclaimed with a whoop of delight which suddenly changed to one of concern.

'There's the site up there, but look, there are police cars everywhere... Christ! and army vehicles.' Although we were still some distance away we could see considerable activity taking place by both army and police.

'Perhaps it's another bomb scare,' I offered. There had been a spate of IRA explosions and reports of suspicious objects in and around the capital, but Jeff was already running, with me in hot pursuit.

As we got closer we could see the area had been cordoned off and a small crowd had gathered.

'What's going on?' Jeff demanded of a bystander.

'They've found a bomb,' declared the man, 'it's been hidden on the building site.'

Jeff's expression changed to horror and he ran to the nearest policeman.

'Go back behind the cordon, please sir, the army are operating a controlled explosion.'

'Not near my bloody suitcase they ain't,' snarled Jeff, but the words died in his throat.

As we looked across the expanse of open ground which separated police and army from the half-finished buildings, there appeared a remote-controlled robot backing out of a small, half-finished toilet, dragging ... a battered suitcase.

I shall never forget the expression on Jeff's face as long as I live. For a few seconds he stood motionless, and then without warning let out a bloodcurdling scream and raced across the open ground, with the horrified shouts of law and army alike in his wake.

'Get off my fucking suitcase, you mechanical pig,' he screamed, hurling himself at the robot, knocking it on to its side.

The world stood still as Jeff proceeded to rain blows and kicks at the robot, which by now was making the most peculiar noises and kicking its steel legs in the air.

Then all hell broke loose with blue and khaki emerging from everywhere and descending without mercy upon a wildly kicking Jeff. As they dragged him towards the parked police cars he was still somehow connected to the mass of metal which had recently been a robot, although it was now being towed ignominiously through the dust. Suddenly I was released from the spell. The whole thing could have only taken a minute but I had been paralysed with surprise, and I raced into the fray.

'He's my mate, leave him alone you bastards … the case is ours … let go, you fucking flatfoot.'

In no time at all we were unceremoniously bundled into a patrol car and it began to force its way through the now gathering crowd.

It was at this point that I noticed, through the window of the car, the workers from the building site who had obviously been evacuated when the case had been found. One was on his knees holding his sides in agony caused from laughter, several had sought support from each other as tears of mirth rolled down their faces. I pointed them out to Jeff.

'Huh, wasn't their bloody suitcase,' he mumbled.

Jeff and I had much in common … both of us were musicians and both alcoholics. Our lives had run a parallel course that was so similar we could have been brothers. We even looked alike and soon we became inseparable. If you saw one the other was not far away, and we were given the nicknames of Smith and Jones – characters in a popular television series. Our personalities and ideas just 'clicked' and the source of our first business venture was a large city restaurant.

We had both started work there cleaning and tidying up the astounding amount of rubbish which accumulates in a large restaurant, sweeping passages and floors, cleaning away glasses and many other odd jobs. Our pay was a couple of pounds a day plus 'seconds'. 'Seconds' when applied to drinks, literally means what it says. Large quantities of wine and spirits are sold to business people in a hurry and, inevitably, some drink is left behind in both glasses and bottles. We would tip all of these into a plastic container and filter the entire amount through an ordinary beer filter and bottle the concoction in empty lemonade bottles. Some days it tasted better than others, but generally it was pretty unusual to say the least. The taste, however, did not matter to us, we were drinking for effect.

In no time at all we became well known in all the pubs around the immediate area of the hostel, and many of the office workers and bankers who frequented them knew us by name. One evening as we were enjoying a drink, I put one of four bottles of 'seconds' on the counter to ease the weight in my overcoat pocket. A merchant banker, who nearly always bought us a drink, grabbed hold of the concoction and, holding it up to the light, exclaimed, 'That looks like a drop of good stuff, Smith. What is it?'

'Well, er... er... it's er...' The question had caught me on the wrong foot but my brain was working overtime. '...as a matter of fact an old friend of ours brews it himself – he's a genius.' The top was off now and our educated friend was sniffing expertly at the liquid within.

'I say, Smith, would you possibly allow me to taste it?'

Jeff was taking more than just a passing interest in the proceedings and had broken off his conversation with the landlord. He had 'cottoned on' and was poised to help if the occasion arose.

The landlord joined the proceedings and produced a clean spirit glass for the gentleman. A generous measure was poured and the banker raised the glass in the manner of a professional wine-taster.

'I say, this is really rather good ... hmmm ... do you think I could buy a bottle or two from you?'

I could hardly contain my surprise, but at the same time I was a bit wary. Jeff and I could drink anything to solve our problem, but we could not guarantee the quality and taste of the stuff – or could we?

'We pay one pound a bottle,' Jeff chipped in, and the price seemed right to me. If we could sell every bottle we were able to fill, we knew we could make some real money. Naturally we would have to be careful when the 'seconds' were filtered. The banker decided to buy two bottles and we were in business.

In the weeks that followed we could have poisoned the entire office and banking population in and around Liverpool Street, but we did not hear of any complaints. The bottles were properly washed and we made sure that none of the alcohol contained a mixer (i.e. peppermint, blackcurrant, ginger, etc.) but I am sure the health inspectors would have been appalled. The mixture consisted of different wines – irrespective of colour or whether they were sweet or dry – sherry, port and quite often spirits were thrown in for good measure. We had no way of knowing the proof percentage of our product, but it had a quick kick. The taste, in Jeff's memorable phrase, was 'hauntingly attractive'. Thanks to the money from satisfied customers, Jeff and I were able to purchase a steady supply of drink of our own choosing. For a time withdrawal was banished.

One day we were out walking, trying to think of another money-making venture, when we saw a street busker and stopped to watch and listen.

'Ever tried that, Nick?'

I shook my head without looking at him, my eyes riveted on the bag of coins the busker's side-kick was holding.

'Well, do you think we could give it a try?' Jeff dug me in the ribs and the look of excitement in his eyes proved infectious.

'I suppose it might be worth a try, but we'll need a guitar – got any ideas?' I looked at him expectantly and this time he nodded.

'Leave it to me.'

The following day Jeff returned with a guitar. He had done a deal with a junior manager at the restaurant where he worked. That evening we planned our busking debut and decided to try out our act on Sunday morning in Petticoat Lane. It proved to be something of an anticlimax.

One thing I discovered was that busking was nothing like entertaining as I knew it. It was a different art form and only practice, and watching fellow-buskers, would enable me to perform successfully. As the basics were the same, I picked it up very quickly.

There was a great deal of loyalty among the busking fraternity and the 'good pitches' were split fairly among those who were officially recognised by the established acts. I have made big money in my life but Jeff and I had never been

(*left*) Me at school aged eight.
(*right*) With my dad, mum and sister Judith at the seaside.
(*below*) Many years later - and six months into my recovery - I returned to the places where I fought my alcoholism to capture something of life on the streets in the following photographs.

(*left*) My bed, still remaining six months after my last drink, in a shack in Spitalfields.
(*above*) Our dining table by the Spitalfields fire, complete with jacket potatoes.

(*left*) The Salvation Army Social Services office in Petticoat Lane, scene of the answer to many a prayer.

(*below*) My last Salvation Army bed stands to the left of the pillar in the foreground.

(*right*) The house from which I narrowly escaped with my life is now covered in corrugated iron.

(*left*) Disused boiler-house steps at the bottom of which I was found with multiple injuries after my battle with the rats.

(*above*) The infamous alley where Jack the Ripper's victim Mary Kelly was found provided many nights' kip for me.

(*left*) This is where I last saw Harry's Hat - and Harry.
(*above*) I spent many nights here - a wreck within a wreck.

Old Tom often joked on nights he slept here that he knew he would one day make it into Parliament.

Every dosser was once someone's baby.

(*above*) Meeting Prince Charles;
(*left*) with my MBE
at Buckingham Palace.

involved in making such crazy money as we did in the months that followed. It was never our intention to make a fortune – only to make cash for booze – and to this end we were magnificently successful. I never busked for more than half an hour and we never earned less than six pounds – more often it was over ten – and, then every evening, we sat in the bar in Liverpool Street Station watching the television in comfort.

We made many friends among our fellow 'street artistes' and discovered that the majority lived in rooms dotted around the city. A few, however, had a small hideaway on the wharf by London Bridge. This particular crowd became our close friends and soon afterwards we moved in with them.

If you could look over the parapet, at the place we fondly called No 2 London Bridge, you would marvel at the difficulties involved in reaching the wharf from the steps that led down to the water. There was no direct route. We had to climb down the stair-rails and jump about four feet – to avoid the drop into the Thames – before landing on a concrete slipway. None of us ever came to grief but, on the other hand, none of us ever did it entirely sober.

When Jeff and I arrived, we started to make the place more home-like by adding bits and pieces we had bought at various jumble sales. By introducing a compulsory 'silver' collection we were able to buy a small Calor gas stove and a few saucepans. Mattresses followed, in varying conditions, and blankets – until the only thing that was missing were the deeds to the property.

One of the lads had a portable television, and there were three or four radios, but we had to keep the volume to a minimum. No one ever knew we lived there and we were never interfered with – except for a friendly postman – and he only called once. The postman's visit will live in my memory as one of the most comical situations I have ever witnessed, although I was very angry at the time.

One morning Jeff and I were about to climb back up the stairs when a voice hailed us. Seeing the uniform, I was about to run for cover when Jeff's voice floated reassuringly across no man's land.

'It's okay, just the postman for me.'

I was amazed to watch him take an envelope from the postman and proudly hand it to me. The envelope was addressed to:-

Jeff Parker, Esq,
No.2 London Bridge.

When we reached the road, he pointed to the wall where he had written the number in chalk.

'You bloody idiot! Do you want the law around here ... ?'

A very chastened Jeff reluctantly rubbed away the chalk. The day before, in a moment of madness, he had simply posted an empty envelope to himself.

Life under London Bridge could have gone on indefinitely, but we were ambitious and forever becoming involved in incredible escapades. One evening, having finished our stint at the Liverpool Street Underground earlier than usual, we decided to try another pub. There were quite a few to choose from and we headed down Middlesex Street towards Aldgate East. A coach driver – recognisable by his badge – stopped us and asked about parking facilities for coaches visiting 'Dirty Dick's' public house. We told him that coaches always parked outside when visiting the pub. He explained that there were six coachloads of American visitors in search of local colour.

'Tell you what, mate,' I said in a friendly manner, 'we'll put on a street show for them as they get off the coach – it'll make their night. If you could say a few words to encourage them to part with a few bob we'll cut you in ... '

He grinned and said, 'Okay, I'll do my best... See you in five minutes.'

Then followed the craziest busker bonanza of all time.

Every tourist on the six coaches paid out in staggering amounts and, inside twenty minutes, crowds of dancing Yanks were causing so many traffic obstructions it was embarrassing. Jeff had given up holding out his hat and was stuffing notes and silver into every pocket. Both of us posed with people for various photographs, and the flash-bulbs were going at such a rate that the whole area was as bright as day. Then came the law!

Jeff saw them first and neither of us paused for breath until we were well away from the thronging crowds. We found a quiet pub, in an Aldgate back street, and excitedly counted the proceeds. We knew we had hit the jackpot – but neither of us was prepared for the staggering total that had been thrust at Jeff in only three-quarters of an hour.

Bundles of crumpled notes were pulled out and the table in the deserted bar was covered with papermoney. The night air had been decidedly chilly during the act and I had wondered vaguely why Jeff had placed his overcoat over his shoulder. The reason was that the huge inside pockets were loaded with coins of every denomination and must have weighed a ton.

'How the hell did you run with that coat, Jeff?' It seemed incredible that he had sprinted nearly four hundred yards carrying that weight.

'It just goes to show what you can do if you need to do it badly enough,' he mused thoughtfully. 'You know, I reckon we've got over a hundred quid here. They were a rich crowd and a generous one. I don't know what the driver said to them, but he certainly ought to get a handout.'

I began to think about this, but Jeff's voice interrupted my line of thought.

'...hundred and two, three, four, five, six. There you go, one hundred and six pounds in notes and four large pocketfuls of change, mainly silver. My God, Nick! No one will ever believe it. I can hardly believe it myself. I bet no one's ever had a lucky break like that while standing on a street corner holding a guitar!'

I had to agree, but I was still concerned about the coach driver.

'You're right, Jeff, but as you say, it didn't just fall at our feet. That driver buttered-up the party for us, that's for sure, and we're gonna give him a note or two.'

The landlord accepted the forty-odd pounds' worth of

change and, after downing a couple of large brandies, we set off in the direction of Dirty Dick's.

The coaches were still parked in the same place, but Jeff and I slipped discreetly into the Woodin Shades on the opposite corner. I looked around for someone I knew. Luckily there were several faces from the Salvation Army Hostel nearby and I approached someone I knew fairly well.

'Do us a favour, Jock, go and tell the driver of the first coach that a couple of guys want to see him. If he's not in the bus he'll be in Dirty's bar – and there'll be a few drinks for you when you get back.'

Jock left without a word and I rejoined Jeff, who was standing at the counter. Minutes passed and nothing was said, but I knew a lot of similar thoughts were passing through our minds – aided by the warm glow from the brandy.

'Hello, lads, how did it go then?'

We swung around together and saw the cheerful face of our coach driver friend with Jock hovering behind him. I slipped the messenger a note, and soon the three of us were laughing and joking over the night's events.

'Never in all the years I've bin driving coaches have I ever seen anything like it – they loved you! Do you know, they're still talking about it in the pub next door.'

It appeared that he had told the tourists we were friends of his and that we were part of the real London of the sixties – and had to rely on their generosity for our livelihood!

'I'm glad you turned out to be a good act. If you'd bin rubbish they'd have lynched me after the terrific build-up I gave you.'

He was a jovial character and was particularly interested to hear about some of our adventures. But he sensibly refused the majority of the drinks we wanted to buy him, because of the long drive back. Instead, we gave him a handsome tip and he was delighted.

It had been a highly profitable evening in every way.

17

Rough-house

The following day, in the true alcoholic tradition, Jeff and I awoke early with ghastly withdrawal symptoms and terrible hangovers. Seven a.m. saw us outside the early-opener at Billingsgate Fish Market and, as soon as we got inside, we gratefully relieved our symptoms with a shot of brandy. An hour later we were making plans to use the money to get a flat, somewhere nearby, and the future suddenly seemed very rosy.

Having secured a copy of the evening paper as soon as the early edition came out, we combed the columns for anything suitable. Flats were not as readily available as we had imagined, and certainly not for the amount of cash we had to offer. We had to settle, eventually, for a small ground-floor bedsit in East London.

The plan was basically a good one and we started off with the best of intentions. We thought we could begin to live a normal life; but it was only wishful thinking, and we remained pathetically addicted to drink.

By the time we had settled into our new surroundings and purchased all the items necessary to be independent, we were practically broke. There was just enough money for one night's drinking. After that it was back to busking, or a 'casual' at one of the restaurants.

We tried several of the local pubs and found one we particularly liked. It had a friendly atmosphere and soon we were being hailed as 'personalities' when we did our act on the small stage at the far end of the bar. Halfway through one evening's performance, Jeff took me aside and reminded me of our poor cash-in-hand position and the fact that I was supposed to be the financial wizard in the partnership. If he meant conman he was right, for I was already working on something.

A sound engineer we knew had mentioned, on a couple of occasions, that the background music systems he serviced were only a small part of his job. He told me he could probably get a second-hand amplifier that would suit my purpose for around twenty pounds. With this figure in mind, I approached the landlord. I outlined my plan to him, explaining what would be involved. I knew he was looking for a good act for his pub and I also knew that I was far better than the normal 'run-of-the-mill' acts that were available. The 'con' hinged on the fact that he wanted me and I needed an amplifier before I could perform regularly. The twenty pounds was soon in my pocket and an excellent night was had by all... But, the following day, I awoke with only fifteen pounds and the knowledge that, if the chances of obtaining an amplifier for twenty were remote, for fifteen they were impossible.

We were scheduled to play at the pub the following Saturday – but that was six days away. Alcohol performed its miraculous act of making anything of consequence seem unimportant, and Jeff and I found peace in its company. During the week we worked hard at the restaurant and even managed to fit in four hours of busking. By Saturday afternoon we had earned and spent about ninety pounds, a grim example of the cost and extent of our drinking bouts. The original twenty pounds was completely forgotten.

At a party of buskers that evening we managed to sink vast

amounts of booze and, when we returned to our room early on Sunday morning, I was conscious that a lot of people would be annoyed by our absence from the pub the night before. Later that day we went to a different pub for some liquid courage before 'facing the music'; it proved to be a mistake. We had hardly swallowed our first drink when two 'heavies' – friends of the landlord – came through the door and straight up to where we were sitting.

'You got till ten o'clock tonight to come up with the money!'

It was the larger of the two who spoke and it was all that was said before they turned and left.

'My God! What a mess! How are we gonna get out of this one?' Jeff's voice was almost a whisper and I couldn't think of anything to say. 'What about your friend who keeps the pub in Hackney...wouldn't he lend you a score?'

Jeff's suggestion made sense. There was such a friend, and a chance he might come up trumps. I was prepared to try anything and the first step was to dress for the part.

The only way Jeff and I could dress reasonably well was to pick the best from our combined wardrobes, it was an amusing situation. Jeff always kept one pair of trousers in reserve and I had a shirt that could be worn with the only tie available. We always bought the same cheap shoes and, as I wore out the right and Jeff the left, it was just possible to look presentable. There was just one problem. All the time I was wearing Jeff's trousers he was constantly telling me to look after them ... watch the creases ... be careful with that cigarette!

Looking reasonably respectable, I set off to see my publican friend. When I arrived back, at a pre-arranged pub, all I had managed to borrow was a tenner. It wasn't enough to solve anything, but it was enough to buy the means to deaden any pain that might be inflicted, if our former 'friends' arrived to collect.

'Do you think they'll come?' asked Jeff, mournfully.

I managed a smile and we drank up and began to walk home.

'Change out of my trousers in case they do, Nick. Whatever happens, I don't want them ripped or knocked about...'

We knew someone had been in our bedsit as soon as we

opened the door. The radio was gone! We had never replaced the missing bolt on the sash-window and anyone could gain entry if they tried. Jeff was just going to secure the lock when a voice we recognised demanded that we open the door.

'Now we're for it!' exploded Jeff, backing away. 'Take my bloody trousers off!'

Just as I thought he might attempt to remove them forcibly, the door burst open and the debt-collecting agency arrived in force. There were four of them, and they didn't say much as they went to work. Incredibly, Jeff was still demanding that I remove his trousers as we tried to defend ourselves.

I had been suffering from 'wind' all evening and, just prior to the arrival of our unwanted visitors, I had diagnosed acute diarrhoea. By this time my innards were grossly overloaded and my bowels under terrific pressure. I actually begged my assailants, who were now putting the boot in, to allow me to go to the toilet. I even promised to return to the fray immediately I had finished; but they didn't have any manners.

Suddenly, with no apology, there was an ear-splitting fart and the air was poisoned with the most awful smell I had ever experienced. Everyone stopped as the whole room became contaminated.

'Christ! Let's get out of here ...' pleaded an assailant, and in seconds the room was cleared and silent.

I looked up and saw Jeff's face covered with blood. I moved very slowly into a sitting position, I was badly battered but my immediate concern was with the humiliating mess in Jeff's trousers.

'Are my trousers okay?' he asked and then, in the same breath, 'what's that bloody awful stink?'

I looked up at him miserably and then down to the evil-smelling mess that was rapidly discolouring his favourite trousers. Painfully I slunk off to the loo, thinking that the real culprit was the wide variety of booze that I had put away over the last twenty-four hours.

Jeff's comments, when he learned the fate of his trousers, are just not repeatable.

It was a sobering shock when I saw my face and neck. I was

black-and-blue and someone had used a knife. Both my eyes were closed except for minute slits. A kindly, middle-aged divorcee, who lived upstairs, had heard the noise and was now appalled at the physical damage that met her gaze. She fetched a first-aid kit from her flat and began to bathe our wounds.

'You'll have to go to hospital, Smith' (it was now routine to use the Smith-Jones tag for all outsiders). 'You may have a fracture ... I don't like the look of you at all.'

Many times, as she gently bathed my face, she repeated her words; but I refused to go.

After we were both in bed I couldn't get to sleep because my head ached terribly. The pain across my forehead and at the pit of my stomach – where I had been kicked – were almost beyond endurance. The following day I could only walk with considerable pain. Jeff had been lucky, but only in comparison. He did his share of suffering.

By lunchtime, I felt that something was seriously wrong and set out, with Jeff's help, to a nearby hospital. After being X-rayed – and found to have three fractures of the skull, concussion and damaged kidneys – I was admitted immediately. There was also internal bleeding.

I was kept in hospital for a month, during which time I wrote three or four letters to Jeff without receiving a reply. I knew we had lost our digs as there was no one to pay my rent, so, on my discharge, I reported to Scarborough Street Labour Exchange without going back. I asked around all the old haunts, but he had gone. It had been a short but deep friendship and I was sad to think that Jeff had gone his own way without at least saying goodbye ... but he would have his reasons.

My hospital stay had done one thing for me that I had no control over – I had completely dried out. Thanks to the pain-killers, there had been almost no withdrawal symptoms. I decided to remain sober, permanently, once again.

18

A Shadow from the Past

The casual work I did in smart city lunch-club restaurants is, to the alcoholic floating population, what employment contracts are to the city slicker.

As a 'casual' kitchen porter in Fenchurch Street in the City of London, washing saucepans so large I could climb aboard, I laboured less than twenty yards from those lunching who drove Jaguars, Mercedes and worked the Stock Exchange or similar.

Walls, partitions, or delicate drapes diplomatically separated us, but what would they think if they knew the glass that held their gin and tonic had been washed by someone sleeping in a sewer or under a viaduct?

There would be a daily queue of all those hopeful for a day's wages resembling those of the worst days of the General Strike. It was pitiful witnessing a poor soul pretending to be fitter or more sober than he actually was – standing to attention, sticking out a chest, forcing a smile and all because he was a slave to the bottle.

On this particular day I could see the man next to me had once been handsome, in a Mediterranean sort of way, but was now unable to function in normal society, even less follow the fashion. His face was covered in sores that wept like his mother's tears and he would never again walk through my home town in full regalia with a happy carefree heart.

So far from home, its warmth and the camaraderie of village life. Fate had dealt a deadly hand, Peter Elliot and I stood together in ignominy. It hurt me to turn my head in his direction, my legs were raw and my armpits chapped from lack of good food and simple healthcare. I balanced an enormous pan on the edge of the sink that separated us and told him my name.

'I know,' he said looking away.

'How did it happen?' I asked helplessly.

He began to sob silently, put on a filthy coat and shuffled away, unable to face his shame.

One week later he was found murdered – Peter had finally made his escape.

19

Old Tom

Peter Elliot and I did not represent the alcohol tragedy exclusively by any means. Many a quiet tear have I shed in memory of Old Tom ... I never knew his second name. Dressed in a grimy shirt, holed pullover, baggy dirty trousers and an overcoat that reached to the ground, he looked more like an advertisement for 'what not to buy' than a drop-out from society.

I first met Tom on a winter morning in London's Spitalfields Market. Seven drop-outs were gathered, shivering, around a fire they had built out of broken vegetable cases. As I approached them on that bitter morning, I still had vestiges of youthful pride and the memories of past success. Seeking some warmth, I joined the circle around the fire and, at that moment, realised I was truly one of them. And yet I thought I still had a choice. For me it could be a temporary situation but, for them, there was no choice – old age barred the way.

'Got a fag?' were Tom's first words to me.

I had a new packet of kingsize that I had bought from money recently earned and I handed them over. Tom struggled, with shaking, grimy hands, to pull a cigarette from the tightly packed contents. I had to help him and then, after handing them round to the others, lit one myself.

'What's your name?' I asked.

'Tom,' he told me, and the silence continued, broken only by the crackle of the fire.

My memory raced back over the years and I compared this pathetic setting with a family Guy Fawkes party. I recalled in those happier times we would gather round the bonfire, eating sandwiches and black pudding, watching, fascinated, as fireworks exploded all around and then rushing indoors, as the fire died down, to the warm refuge of the sitting room ...

There was no retreat from this fire. My back was warm now, but my face and front were cold beyond description. I turned round and faced the glowing embers, surveying the other faces beside me.

A black man stood opposite. Jamaican, I thought. Grey ash picked up by the wind flecked his hair and his face was gaunt and expressionless. It crossed my mind to ask him what the hell he was doing in a climate like this, but dismissed the idea as futile. He was probably thinking the same thing anyway.

Just then, I again became aware of Tom, he was shaking – uncontrollably. I had seen withdrawal – God! I had suffered enough myself – but this was different.

'You okay?' I asked. The question seemed ridiculous as he was obviously bad.

'Probably pneumonia again,' he managed. 'I hope it is – they take you in for that.'

His remark made me realise the futility of some people's lives.

'Can I buy you a cup of tea?' I suggested.

Tom lifted his head and looked at me. They were friendly eyes, steely blue, but the pain of too many years of hardship showed. His face was lined as if from being permanently screwed up to avoid the cold, and his thick eyebrows sprouted in all directions like straw left over by a West Country thatcher. He nodded and attempted a smile then, without a word, he walked towards a row of shops and turned right. Twenty yards away I saw the café.

Painfully, Tom eased his fragile frame into a vacant seat and I went up to the counter. A few minutes later he gratefully sipped the tea. The hands were steadier now and I detected a slight return of colour to his greying cheeks.

'What did you do this for?' His tone was not unfriendly, just curious.

'Maybe I might be grateful to someone myself one day,' I said uncertainly. A few more minutes passed and then, without thinking, I said, 'How did you come down to this?' My words seemed somehow empty and almost offensive, but my guest did not seem to mind or, if he did, chose not to show it.

'I got wounded in the Second War – bullet in the lung. Never could work properly after being demobbed. The wife went off with some guy more able to provide than me, and I couldn't find roots after that. Been all over the country, mostly on foot.'

That was the longest speech Tom had made so far and I felt encouraged; besides, any sort of conversation was keeping me out of the nearest boozer.

'How did you cop it?' I asked.

He sighed gently as if trying to remember, then replied, 'Funny, no one ever asked before – not since I came out of the Army that is. The wife, Gladys her name was, never asked, only used it to accuse me of being half a man.'

Silence reigned again but I did not prompt him ... It was obvious he had not finished.

'It wasn't long after D-Day,' he said slowly, 'about the middle of July I was with the Second Army. I had landed with the rest on the morning of 6th June, just over a month before. It was such terrible fighting ... so much bloodshed. It all seems so unnecessary now I look back, especially the state the country has got itself into again. It was Hitler in my day, now it's Communism ... There'll always be something I suppose...'

The steely blue eyes gazed into space for a few seconds.

'Funny thing was,' he continued, 'I was in action in 1940 and never got a scratch all the way through. Got captured once with

twenty of my pals. Woke next morning and the enemy had gone
… left us … didn't ever find out why. Two days later we
rejoined our own lads. July, yes July…' he continued, 'Hill 112
they called it. Monty was there, always admired that man. He
sent us towards the Hill from the Salient across the Orne. Not
long afterwards all the British formations West of Caen became
involved. Bloody, bloody fighting. We didn't know at the time,
but we were only a diversion … the main attack was to come
from the east and south. We lost hundreds of men, about four
thousand in all I think …'

I marvelled at his knowledge and the obvious authenticity of
his story.

'The main offensive had a code name, "GOODWOOD" it
was, always remember it 'cos of the race course. Brought about
Rommel's end as a leader. He was in a staff car and an R A F
pilot opened fire on it and he was badly wounded. Never
fought again. Didn't know about it at the time of course, we
heard after. I put the dates together and realised that he caught
it about the same as me. My lot came during the advance on
Hill 112. Shells bursting all around us for days, but I had to
catch a soddin' bullet … Don't remember all that much …
just the force of it hitting me like a fist, if you know what I
mean. Then I coughed blood, couldn't breathe properly and
finally just blackness.

'I woke up in a Military Hospital about three days later, and
soon after that I was shipped back to England. The war was
nearly over anyway and I had done my bit. I suppose you could
say I gave the best years of my life … the years when you young
ones were courting and going to the pictures … '

I reflected on the last time a decent girl had taken an interest
in me and tried to remember the last film I had seen …

'Does the budget stretch to another cuppa, son?'

'Glad of the company,' I replied and went for the tea. Old
Tom was not bullshitting me – I could sense that a mile off –
and his story was really interesting.

Sipping his tea and choosing his words carefully, Tom began
again.

'I was in a hospital, in England then, for about six months. The wife didn't visit at first. I heard later she had been with someone else while I was away. Strange, really, I didn't blame her. I had been away for five years ... Too much to expect a woman to take, don't you think?'

I shrugged.

'Well, the marriage never really got off the ground the second time around, we seemed like two strangers. Somehow it went on for another three years but she left in the end. Good job we didn't have a family, but I often wonder what it would be like if I had a son or a daughter ... '

I contemplated his last remark and my thoughts wandered to my own daughter. Eight years old now, I thought, I hadn't seen her for four years. Every Christmas I had the best intentions, but it always ended the same – hopelessly drunk.

Tom broke into my thoughts.

'Since then I've just gone from bad to worse. Up in court for petty theft, vagrancy and being drunk. I've had the lot, meths, surgical spirit, rendered boot polish, aftershave ... '

He noticed the expression on my face.

'Yes, lad, aftershave – they're all alcohol-based. That aftershave rots your guts worse than anything, only good thing you can say about it is that it makes your breath smell nice.'

I smiled at the grim humour in what he had said. Tom, however, did not see the funny side.

'... And neither would you if you had my stomach,' he said.

I sympathised.

'Trouble with drink is that there is no cure ... You've got to give it up altogether. But if you've sunk as low as me there's nothing left, no incentive to want to be any different.'

He looked at me sorrowfully.

'I know you've got a problem son, recognise it while you still have a chance. You've no need to deny it.'

I closed my mouth.

'If you accept it now, son, you're still young enough to straighten out your life and get a good job. I can see you've got a brain ... You may even find a girl and get wed. It's a sure fact that you won't attract a decent one at the moment ...

'Look,' he continued in earnest, 'how much money have you got in the world?'

I showed him.

'There you are!' he cried 'Three pounds more than me. Now, what's the difference between us? I'll tell you ... Your youth, and that's all, my son ... just your youth.'

I was shaken by his outburst and numbed by the truth – the naked truth.

There was a silence, except for the clatter of the cups coming from the kitchen some distance away. He rose to go.

'Thanks for the tea, son, remember what I said.'

I only saw Tom once after that. It was the day they carried him out of the hostel on a stretcher.

Even in death there was no rest for Tom – to save space his coffin was buried vertically, in an unmarked pauper's grave.

20

Santa's Grotty

December arrived, I was still in a Salvation Army Hostel, actively alcoholic and naturally unemployed. On the twentieth I telephoned my father with a coin I had found on the pavement, and asked him if I could come home just for Christmas Day. He said no and would not accept the charge when the money ran out.

I was scruffy as I recall it, but not dirty, and spent many hours that week wandering around gaily decorated shops and stores, bewildered by and large by my exclusion from the festivities.

It was dark at four o'clock and I recall clearly noticing the warm glow of a log fire and the glitter of decorations and Christmas-tree lights through an uncurtained window of a city home. A family were sat around and a large television screen beckoned an audience. I gazed transfixed; what was different with me that I could have none of this?

I was glad I could have a drink now and again, it was at least a comfort and it also kept out the cold. I pondered on my lot, confused as to why I was different. People seemed to like me at first, I could tell from the way they joined in when we had a good drink. However, they always avoided me from then on and never again made contact. Of course I could not remember everything the next morning so I presumed they had been offended by something I had said.

Jobs, always assuming I could get one, never lasted more than a few days and often only a few hours. I realised it was because occasionally I fell asleep on the job, but more frequently it was because they did not like my opinions on various things, or the way I explained things or offended them. I was slightly put out by the effect alcohol had on me, I did seem to be more affected than most people around me, but everyone drank so I attached little importance to it. Then, just before Christmas I got lucky. I was in a city departmental store by Santa's Grotto when the poor old man was taken ill leaving a queue of unseen kids. A smart man, obviously the manager, seemed panic-stricken and without hesitation I stepped forward and offered my services. 'I'm out of work,' I explained, 'you could soon make me up and stick a beard on and if you like me I'll carry it through.' He considered only for a moment and I was hustled into the staff-room and painted and rouged by a couple of female staff members and dressed in the familiar garb.

The job was really quite splendid. I had a stack of toys at my feet and the store had laid on a glass of sherry on a silver tray for 'Mum' which I offered her from a stock of fifteen bottles strategically placed where I was perched at the top of the stairs with my back to the banisters. I felt obliged to join each mum in a glass of 'festive' and after a couple of hours I ran out of sherry. It may have been this irksome aggravation which made me lose my patience somewhat, but I think with hindsight it was more likely because the child on my knee decided to have a pee.

I later explained to the police that I did not say, 'Take your shitty-arsed pissy kid and chuck it in the fucking river.' I maintained it was not my fault if the banisters were of such bad workmanship that they collapsed when I leant against them and I, together with twenty thousand pounds' worth of Christmas-tree lights and display stock, fell twenty feet to the landing on the floor below. I explained to the station sergeant that I was a member of an espionage ring and had been set up by the CIA.

He obviously believed me because he told me to go away, or words to that effect, and celebrate Christmas in Iceland or Russia, so I wandered out into the cold night air and spent the rest of Christmas looking through other people's windows.

21

Death Wish

Something woke me up. I stared into the blackness searching for whatever had aroused me, my ears straining in an attempt to catch even the slightest sound. I felt a movement on my clothes and, immediately, there was the cold clinging feeling of fear. Another movement, and then again. I could feel the firm pressure of small feet as the thing made its way up my body towards my exposed face. Suddenly I could stand it no longer and, lashing out, flung the bedclothes on to the floor and dived towards the wall where the light switch was located. I seemed to hang in mid-air before crashing to the floor. No light switches under a viaduct, no bedclothes either, just a few old newspapers and bits of cardboard.

There was fur against my face and hands, and it was moving. My fingers gripped tightly around the struggling intruder and instantly I was paralysed with fear. There was not just one, but hundreds, and they were attacking me with ever-increasing ferocity, as though attempting to free the thing that I held tightly in my hand. I got to my feet, struggling, feeling the creatures in my hair, face and eyes. In desperation I groped the air then I was overcome and fell on my knees clawing at the evil fur. Then they started to take shape in the darkness. Slowly at first, and then with gathering certainty, the fur – that before I could only feel – became blood-red spiders with eyes that protruded on stalks from their incredibly ugly bodies.

They were everywhere – some as big as a man's head – and they formed a wide circle with their evil eyes fixed on me. My hands were covered with blood and, although I could not see my face, I knew it was badly cut and scratched. My eyes were burning and the blood in my mouth tasted salty. I felt something razor-sharp slash at my eyes and again I fell to the floor blinded and completely at the mercy of my tormentors ...

Then quite suddenly there was silence, the spiders, the blood and the horror had gone and I was standing shivering on Skid Row. It was yet another encounter with the horrific hallucinations that can be induced by a colossal intake of alcohol.

There was a crumb of comfort in the all-too-familiar sight of the burning fire and fellow down-and-outs huddled closely together. No one spoke. A bottle, which was being passed round without question or comment, eventually found its way to me. I swigged gratefully and looked at my companions. I knew their faces well enough for we had stood together for hours, many times, and yet we did not know each others' names, where we came from or how we had sunk to our present plight. The occasional words that were uttered were only incoherent obscenities.

I spent an hour or more searching for wood and returned with sufficient supplies to keep the fire going through the night. The heat made a cold night endurable, but I slept fitfully. Before morning I decided, yet again, that death was the only way I would ever find peace and, as I was unable to kill myself using a direct method, I determined to do so indirectly – by continuing to drink!

A period of time elapsed. It could have been days or weeks – and it was filled with pain and suffering. My existence would have beggared the adjective 'twilight'. I was drinking rubbish alcohol again and throwing-up with painful regularity. Filthy liquid was among my vomit, together with slivers of plastic-like substance which were almost certainly caused by the alcohol-based lacquers that we habitually drank. My body was continually racked by terrible aches and, in my few moments of awareness, I prayed that I might die.

One day a face in the circle did not return from his ramblings and the word went round that he was dead. Well, at least he had gone to a better place – and I cried. Not for the poor bugger's passing, but because I was still alive!

I became weaker and could no longer forage to refuel the fire. I sensed that the end could not be far away and discovered that there was a basic animal urge, deep within me, to find a quiet place to lie down and die in peace. As darkness fell and the streets became empty, I left my silent companions and made my way, slowly and agonisingly, in the general direction of an old sewage pipe that I had often used for sleeping. It was about a mile away and offered shelter and a certain degree of warmth.

The pipe was now obsolete but an evil-smelling liquid, that came from deep within the intestines of the city, still trickled along its length. The diameter was large enough to crawl into and I had, previously, smuggled in some plastic beer crates to lie on. I vaguely remember attempting the task of gaining entry to the pipe along the mud of the river bank. I had managed it many times before, but then I had been much stronger. Now, covered from head to foot in slimy mud, I finally made it and collapsed, completely exhausted, on top of the crates.

The sun began to shine ... the clouds rolled away leaving a beautiful expanse of blue and my mother and father welcomed me home. My sister, whom I had not seen for years, put her arms around me with gentle tenderness. All of my old friends were with me, I recognised a comedian whom I had met years ago on the northern club circuit, and then it all began to fade ... I screamed for everyone to come back – not to leave me – but they were in the distance now, waving to me. No matter how I tried I could not get them to return. An enormous black sheet was wrapped around me by invisible hands and then I was enveloped in utter darkness.

22

Resurrection

The situation was familiar: a hospital ward, clean sheets and the smell of antiseptic.

'Hello! It's good to have you back in the land of the living.'

I looked up at the smiling face of a young Chinese nurse and struggled to recollect my thoughts. The full horror of the recent past eluded me.

'Was it as bad as that?' I managed.

'Yes, I'm afraid it was. How do you feel now?'

'I can't see very well.'

'Well, just rest quietly and I'll get someone to come and see you.'

I smiled weakly and closed my eyes. There was plenty to mull over and it was all bad. The more recent events were vague, mixed-up and hazy. I struggled to arrange them into some sort of order and, although I was an old hand at the game, it wasn't easy.

Trying to shift my position in the bed was agony. From the pain in my legs, stomach and chest I realised that, however harmful it might be, I did not acquire such painful injuries from simply drinking rubbishy alcohol.

Looking around, I tried to focus my eyes but everything was blurred and the build-up of pain, deep inside my forehead, forced me to close them.

I had to try and remember clearly ... I felt like a rat in a trap. Rats! Those bloody rats! Memories flooded back ... I had been brought back from that 'final' sleep to find them gnawing at my lower abdomen through my urine-soaked clothes. I remember retreating deeper into the sewer to escape the vermin – only to find myself trapped.

We had faced each other for an interminable age and then I decided I had to make a break. Seconds seemed like minutes and then I hurled myself towards the opening with a strength that I thought had deserted me for ever. But the rats moved with amazing speed and their evil bodies seemed to be all over me.

I shuddered beneath the sheets and, gently, I tried to touch my aching side but it was impossible. I forced my eyes open to examine my hands. They were thickly bandaged. I moved my head from side to side against the pillow ... it too was swathed in bandages.

Despite the pain and the noise in my head, I forced myself to remember what had happened; but I drifted away and came to, writhing in agony, when the same young nurse placed a firm hand on my shoulder and spoke with that soft, musical voice, 'Are you all right? Can I get you anything? The doctor will be here to see you shortly.'

She spoke without expecting an answer, simultaneously rearranging the sheets that were in a complete mess. Then she moved to walk away.

'Please don't go,' I shouted in a whispered croak. 'Tell me when I came here. How did this all happen?' I held my bandaged hands in the air. Spasms of pain shot up and down my arms and pity and concern showed in her beautiful oriental eyes.

'We think you must have been mugged. You were found lying at the bottom of some basement stairs, probably for hours ...'

The accent was definitely Cockney. Nothing was real about

any of this; rats fighting me for territorial rights … Chinese Cockney nurses and now … I had been mugged!

'You are being treated for frostbite,' she continued, without realising just how confused I was already, 'and you must try and lie really still as just to complicate matters you've got a fracture of the skull. Now I must go as I have a lot of work to do … '

'Jesus …' I whispered, as she smiled and turned away in a swirl of starched aprons. I tried to think, to remember, but it was no good. I knew, from bitter experience, that there would be no place in a medical ward for a meths-swigging alcoholic, so I decided to be their victim of a mugging as this explanation gave me the best chance for a possible rehabilitation.

Later a doctor arrived and warned me about 'suspected internal injuries'. I added the information to the list of skull fracture, cuts and frostbite – I wasn't smiling!

'Those animals left you to die,' the doctor continued, 'and, judging from your condition upon admission, you must have been lying in the open for a long time. Do you realise,' he went on, wagging his pen in my direction, 'mugging was unheard of fifteen years ago, and now we have five a day in this hospital alone? If you, and people like you do not stand up in court and get these hooligans jailed, we will never beat them. Anyway, the police will be here to interview you tomorrow.'

The police came; I could remember nothing, and they left. X-rays, X-rays and then more X-rays. Visits in an ambulance to Moorfields Eye Hospital with my Cockney oriental nurse, and never a mention of alcoholism.

'You will have a long illness from which you will recover completely,' she told me on one of my many outpatient visits while waiting my turn in the queue. 'My uncle in China taught me palm-reading; he was a very wise man.' She looked puzzled for a moment as she gazed into my palm and beyond. 'There has been a lot of sadness, but happiness is ahead.'

I thought of my long self-inflicted suffering, but said nothing. She told me something of her life in London. Born of Chinese parents, there was the obvious confusion of growing up and working in a Western environment only to return home to an entirely different culture at the end of each day.

The treatment went on. Injections for this, blood tests for that and, with every day that passed, I became stronger and more confident. Knowing that the day of my discharge was drawing closer, I treasured the security and reliability of hospital life. I knew that I would never have a better chance of saving myself from the horrors of alcoholism. It seemed that from the time I had taken my first drink nothing about my lifestyle had been really normal in the accepted sense of the word. The experts were right when they stated that alcoholism was a progressive disease. I had certainly become progressively worse until I had, finally, wanted to die in that disused sewer. But fate had decreed otherwise. Now I had been given a new opportunity to live a sober and useful existence away from the rat-infested sewers and the condemned buildings that had been my home for too long.

23

Square One

The practical beginning of this new-found opportunity arrived on a beautiful sunny morning in early spring when I walked out of the hospital on to a busy London pavement for the first time in two months. This was the London I loved. The hustle and bustle, the Cockney voices, the indefinable smell of the city and, particularly, the thrill of being in the music capital of the world.

I saw an empty bench overlooking a public garden and sat down. Closing my eyes against the warm sunshine, my mind drifted back over some of the experiences of my past. I had made a career out of having alcohol as a constant companion and, being my own worst enemy, could look back on disaster after disaster. I then began wondering if sleeping rough had been tougher than my various car accidents, or the agony of withdrawal more painful than my being a frequent patient in hospital. Several times I winced with remembered pain, but I managed a smile or two as well. One event, however, stood out from all the others ...

It had been a very bad day towards the end of an even worse

summer, and my general appearance was ghastly. I hadn't eaten properly for weeks and had consumed terrific amounts of rubbish alcohol. My clothes were soaked in urine and smelled of human excrement. An 'advanced' alcoholic-dosser has little or no control over his bowels, constantly passing water and caring very little who sees him. The slightest physical strain is enough to begin a bowel action. There are no solids, only an evil liquid which trickles between the chapped skin and the swollen, bleeding haemorrhoids, to congeal, with the blood, on grimy skin. That day it was my skin.

The party of people enjoying the sights around Piccadilly were full of laughter until they saw me and my filthy outstretched hand.

'Oh, for God's sake, push off, mate. You smell evil!' The whole group stood still and gaped and, through the pain and suffering, I saw Pamela. Once I had taken her out in my new estate car and now there she was, standing close by, and still as pretty as a picture. I was remembering how she had lain in my arms in that other existence when a voice broke into my reverie. 'Come on, Pam! Leave that old tramp alone before you catch something.' The voice belonged to John, I knew him too and most of the others as well. They were all from my home town and obviously on a day or weekend trip. In seconds they were gone, leaving me behind with but one consolation – I had not been recognised.

24

The Princess and the Pauper
Part One

There is a saying: 'You can take the man off the streets but you cannot take the streets off the man.'
I think I have proved this to be not entirely correct, but only just, and not easily.

I had a friend who lived in squats and on occasions would allow me to go with him and wash myself, their one luxury being cold running water. On one such occasion he told me of a vacancy at his place of work. I can recall him clearly, sat on a pile of old newspapers, face shining with enthusiasm, dressed absurdly in a modern evening dress suit, all that necessity bade him retain from his addiction to gambling. There was not a stick of furniture to be seen anywhere and I still puzzle to this day as to how the electric light had remained connected.

It is an impossible job to remove quickly the deeply ingrained trademark that the gutter leaves behind after several weeks with only the sky for a ceiling. I pointed this out to him, plus another minor factor – the only clothes I owned I stood up in and they were only good for the incinerator.

This presented no problem, he had gushed. He worked the day shift, the vacancy was for the night shift, he would return home early on the day I was to attend the interviews – I would attend wearing his suit. To the management my explanation was that I had dressed for the part so they could see me as I presented for work. When I received wages I could buy a suit of my own.

I saw three major problems. The first was that he was six feet tall and wore size ten shoes. I was five feet, eight inches tall and wore size eight shoes. The second was twelve hours was a long time for the person not working to sit in a cold, unheated broken-down squat in his underpants. The third seemed almost minor in comparison. How would the suit stand up to two twelve-hour shifts encasing two separate human forms for anything up to two weeks and still remain fit to serve?

In order to fully understand the ramifications and appreciate the bizarre events that were about to unfold, I will set the scene. To begin, imagine a ladies' and gentlemen's club restaurant with a membership so select it can take years to gain entry. Imagine a clientele that includes the crème-de-la-crème of the stage, theatre and film industry. Those who were not, could lay claim to predominance in the arts, law and even aristocracy. Then imagine me, my friend, the squat and the suit.

The evening grill room was a relatively recent addition to the services available and it was for a vacancy in this department that I was to be interviewed.

I have to concede it went very well all things considered. I was extremely conscious of the two dozen knob pins holding up six inches of material to fit my shorter legs, to say nothing of the screwed up bits of an old tabloid newspaper filling the gap between my toes and where the size tens ended. It was a suit of good quality and I had brushed it until the pile looked new. Its pedigree was certainly to be tested.

'We require you to work two weeks in hand therefore you will receive your first wages at the end of the third week,' said the personnel officer.

Jesus! Three weeks for the two of us in one suit and a freezing squat.

The training went well, superbly in fact. Most of the male and female staff were gay, and thanks to my experience in the entertainment industry where they were in profusion, I got on famously. I admitted my alcohol addiction in confidence to Danny, my immediate superior, who proceeded to confide in everyone else. No malice, simply the mother hen instinct in the 'old queen'.

I have to concede an overwhelming feeling of relief when I purchased my own evening suit upon receipt of my initial wage packet. That night I served the performance of my life.

I had been at the restaurant for six weeks, three of which were living-in respectably in accommodation provided, yet I could still see evidence of vagrancy ingrained upon my body. I sat on my bed in an enormous bath towel having basked in the luxury of deep hot water until I had suddenly become aware it was cold. The calluses were still evident on my feet and there was a dark stain deep into each fingernail, below where a brush could reach. I was more than a little grateful to the 'queen' and his skin-coloured nail varnish. I looked across at a wall mirror and observed the weather-beaten skin on my face which was fading unevenly, leaving a patchwork effect.

At first it had been strange sleeping in a bed. For the first two nights I had lain on the floor but an annoying draught from a gap under the door had given me a runny eye. I do not recall draughts on the streets.

The actual job was amazing. Some nights it was like being at the cinema so famous were the faces; of one face I am constantly reminded even to this day – each time I see a china doll.

I first saw her one terribly stormy night with lightning flashing, thunder crashing like exploding bombs and torrential rain that penetrated everything bar oilskin. I was going about my business and passing through the hallway as she tumbled through the door in a scurry of panic-stricken movement in an effort to avoid the rain. She had failed miserably. Her dress was soaked through, clinging to her body with little respect for her modesty, just confirming that she wore no bra and announcing that her knickers were black. Behind her came her father, who cuddled her with sympathy that was beyond my understanding of paternal affection. He signalled for my assistance and I responded with a 'Can I help you sir?'

I took her to a small private office and gave her a towel. Her hair was long and tied up in a bun, perfectly straight which when let down reached her waist. A waitress colleague joined us and offered a change of clothes; she gracefully declined but asked if a case could be collected from a nearby theatre. In traditional English fashion I made a pot of tea and she drank gratefully without sugar. She was incredibly famous, I suppose too much alcohol too often too young had affected my brain and its ability to function spontaneously, because I did not recognise her. Little by little the face became an image playing a part. Then many parts on big and little screens, then meeting the Queen, on national news at ten and holding awards at major ceremonies, then asking if she could have another cup of tea! And I must not reveal her real name.

It would not be wholly accurate to describe Joanne, as I'll call her, as beautiful, although she was incredibly pretty. Delicate as a porcelain doll, graceful, fascinating and as attractive as any woman I have ever known, I could barely take my eyes off her. Her father was handsome in his own way but I hardly gave him a second glance. He tipped well, but I felt Joanne's smile was sufficient reward and especially reserved for me.

One night I entered the restaurant area from behind the waiters' screen in one swift movement to take their order. I was only slightly ruffled as I realised he was not there and she was sat alone. 'I'm so sorry, I'll come back when your father returns,' I said.

She smiled diamonds and pearls, words were unnecessary. They were regular customers, twice or three times a week. A fortnight later I met her alone in the foyer.

'He's not my father,' she said simply.

'Pardon?' I felt foolish, it was pointless pretending I did not understand. 'I'm really sorry,' I said quickly and meant it genuinely. Her smile said she forgave me – and maybe more … !

25

Douglas No More

Alcoholism is a progressive illness. It begins with the euphoria of the extra confidence, the feeling of well-being, sensations of indestructibility and the conviction that it's okay because everybody does it. It can end in humiliation, degradation and all the horrors of the alcoholic's non-life.

Alcohol is an anaesthetic. All alcoholic drinks contain ethyl alcohol, a powerful drug that slows down the action of your brain and central nervous system.

Contrary to popular belief, alcohol is actually a depressant, not a stimulant. It is very much like the drugs used to put you to sleep for an operation in hospital and was used as an anaesthetic as recently as the Gulf War. This means it affects your mood, judgement, control, speech, coordination and staying power. Arguably all alcohol addicts are voluntarily anaesthetising themselves for as long, and as continually, as they choose to abuse the liquid.

One of the most sinister effects of this is the anaesthetic freezes in time the brain's ability to mature. The result is, when taken away, the alcohol leaves behind an adult with the mental age of whenever the abuse began. Hence, if alcohol abuse began as a daily practice at the age of seventeen and the victim stopped at age forty, you have a forty year old with a mental outlook aged seventeen. For me, who in drink lapsed into a world of Walter Mitty type imaginings, the real world was a very strange place indeed. When drinking, I had spent my life telling anyone who would listen of my friends amongst the rich and famous. I have fought in several of the world's global conflicts and flown for most of the major airlines at one time or another.

When it came to hallucinations I had certainly had my share, yet they were not all unpleasant and some positively entertaining. During one in particular I lunched with Prince Charles and was tempted to tell him when we met some twenty years later.

At some point in my past fantasies I had told a pub audience that I knew Douglas Bader very well and he had taught me to fly. So it was with some surprise that I marvelled at his ability to walk without the slightest sign of a limp when he came into the restaurant for dinner. I had not been alcohol-free very long and I was occasionally susceptible to moments of disorientation now the powerful drug was removed. This was one such moment and I felt quite faint and unsteady as I approached his table.

'Good evening, Mr Bader.'

Kenneth More looked into my eyes steadily through spectacles tinted slightly blue and he spoke calmly and deliberately.

'Could I have the menu please, young man?'

26

The Princess and the Pauper
Part Two

'Would you like to come to Oscars?' It was my boss Danny asking the question in his effeminate, but friendly voice, hand on hip in classic 'queen' style. 'It's the gay club down the road,' he concluded as he went on checking the silver, not even bothering to look up. 'I'm not gay,' I said as if in my defence rather than as an excuse not to go.

'Never mind ducky, you've got to start somewhere,' he said and flounced off.

After being assured that I would be quite safe I decided to go, and laughed sober laughter till I cried for the first time in years. The place was full of characters. The lesbians turned left as they went into the foyer to their sanctum, and the gays to the right, although there was no major territorial embargo. As promised no one bothered me once Danny told them I was straight, but Barry tried to persuade me with enough chutzpah to charm the birds from the trees.

He was an actor, not famous but well respected among his fellow professionals. He played bit parts and did extra work, but came into his own every Christmas as an ugly sister in panto-mimes which he performed with distinction. He was always pulling my leg and one night I shall always remember. He bought me my usual Coke, and with an arm around my shoulder pulled my ear to his lips.

'Did anyone ever tell you you're as pretty as a picture?' he whispered.

We knew each other well by now and his words offered no threat. I looked sideways at him to see if he was laughing at a joke he was about to punchline. Instead, there were tears in his eyes as he said: 'Oh Nicky, I do wish you were normal.'

I was completely sober, his tears probably rooted in one gin too many, but how I kept a straight face I shall never know.

It wasn't long before I discovered that most of the restaurant clientele assumed, and accepted, that many of the staff were gay. Certainly one or two of the diners discussed it from time to time and one night I overheard part of a conversation.

'Is he really?' the voice belonged to Joanne. 'Gosh what a terrible waste!' The last word was uttered just as I passed the table she shared with 'Dad'. It was unfair, but inexplicably I spitefully preferred to think of him in that way. I looked back in her direction as she spoke. I smiled, she blushed, and I knew the reference was to me. I smiled again and pushed away the sweet trolley with a wiggle.

I regretted my action almost at once. To begin with I had no wish to be thought of as gay, more significantly Joanne was beginning to be important to me.

My shift ended at midnight and I was normally in my room above the restaurant by twelve-thirty a.m. Tonight was the same though different, I closed the door behind me, sat in the only chair and dreamt the impossible dream.

It is so hard to describe to a normal and rational world the confusion of a seventeen-year-old's logic existing in the mind of a man old enough to have a ten-year-old daughter. I imagined a youthful, early teenage romance, holding hands and an innocent kiss on the cheek. Anything beyond was unthinkable, that would be to desecrate, to defile, then I thought of Dad, then of course that he wasn't her father but her lover. To think that she would offer anything other than well-mannered courtesy towards the waiter who served her two or three times a week was preposterous. I came back to earth with a bump and looked at my watch, four a.m. I felt relief not related to madness – in a little over three hours I had matured years through the alcohol anaesthetic to which, for now at least, I was no longer a slave.

Nevertheless I wanted to be alone with Joanne. I had no idea why or what I was going to say if the chance presented itself, but I began to look for an opportunity.

When it came it was unexpected and at the time the furthest thing from my mind. 'Dad' had gone to make a telephone call and she left the table where she sat alone and walked slowly towards me.

'I'm not gay,' I said before she'd quite reached me, almost in an effort to pre-empt her making a decision for herself.

'I'm so very very sorry, what I said was unforgivable.' Her accent was upper class, her eyes sincere and I was breathless. 'Would you allow me to buy you a coffee as a sort of peace token?'

Stupidly, I looked towards the percolator and she giggled making me feel even sillier. 'I don't mean here. I'll be at the Arts Theatre Club at three o'clock tomorrow.' With that she returned to her seat and for the rest of the night I walked around in a daze wondering, amongst many things, what I was going to wear.

'It's where all the arty types go, usually to do business or just gossip,' said Danny the queen in answer to my enquiry. We were about the same size and he spent the late night into early morning conducting his own private fashion show with me as the model.

The following afternoon I headed for the venue, vaguely considering the possibility of being recognised from the rear by one of Danny's friends. Joanne was waiting outside signing autographs. I stood about ten yards away trying to look considerate, or well-mannered or I'm not sure what, then she saw me.

'Oh, darling, hi! I'm sorry,' she said turning back to the youngsters holding out bits of paper, 'I've really got to go now, goodbye.'

'Goodbye, Joanne, thank you, goodbye, we'll be here again tomorrow, will you?'

Joanne skipping towards me smiling happily and grabbing the arm of Danny's jacket, made me want to skip too. I felt like a youngster again, in fact we both behaved like a couple of schoolkids for about half an hour, then suddenly she stopped and became serious, even morose.

'Do you love him?' I asked. I was a great deal underweight, not very fit and short of breath. She looked at me for a long time, her eyes unwavering, then she said slowly, 'I don't know, I've never known anyone else.'

'But you're a famous actress, films, television, my God if I didn't know different I'd think I was pissed, er drunk, just being here.'

'What on earth do you mean, Nicholas?' She looked genuinely confused.

I was genuinely confused. 'Well!' I blustered and struggled to find the words. 'People like you go out to night clubs and Harrods and bloody palaces, they don't get lonely and not have boyfriends. And nobody's called me Nicholas since the last time I saw my mother.'

'Michael says you're a man of mystery.' Joanne looked a little more relaxed.

'Who's Michael?' I enquired. 'Oh you mean "Dad". She giggled a giggle I would associate with her for the rest of my life.

'Are you?' she said.

'Am I what?'

'A man of mystery?' she said.

I looked away from her into the past and said: 'More than you'll ever know.'

Joanne and I met often in the months that followed. We walked miles around London streets and picnicked in Hyde Park on several occasions. The culture shock came in mid-summer.

'I'm going home to my parents in Sussex for a long weekend, would you like to come?'

I'd had a middle-class upbringing. Not because the family were wealthy, far from it, their occupations were most definitely working class. Grandmother, on my father's side however, as already said, was of the Herefordshire Basker-villes, one of England's oldest families. Her teachings, standards and traditions had been passed down. This together with my mother's experience as nanny to twins born of a millionaire industrialist, helped me grow up well prepared for the Burtons.

To say I was well received and successful on a personal front would be an understatement. It was halfway through the weekend before I realised the main reason for the over-whelming welcome. Joanne was walking arm-in-arm with her father through the orchard which was just visible from the patio doors. Mrs Burton touched my arm.

'I cannot tell you how delighted we are that Joanne has a friend her own age and one who comes from good stock to boot. Would you like a glass of sherry, or perhaps a lager?'

I shook my head, deciding that she might not like me if I had a drink.

'Do you know that man is older than her father?' she demanded. I wanted to answer, it was not in my make-up to offer only silence, but the thought of 'Dad' touching Joanne filled me with a revulsion that robbed me of words. She held my arm firmly, smiled a sympathetic and under-standing smile, and brushed away an imaginary obstruction. 'He can't hold a candle to you in any department,' she said finally.

As we left Sussex that weekend I felt an elation it's hard to describe. I wanted so much to be part of Joanne's life and I was as captivated by her family as they obviously were by me.

It was Joanne herself who ruined the moment.

'I shall see you tomorrow night,' she said. For a second it did not register, then I realised she meant the restaurant, which meant she was seeing 'him'.

The following night we stole two minutes in the foyer after they had dined. She stood under a portrait of the actor Leslie Howard and said in a whisper, 'I'll see you tomorrow same time.' I looked up at Howard, he stared back, the shadow of a smile playing on his lips, his eyes firmly fixed on mine.

Perhaps he knew something I didn't because the following day I rang my home and, as a result, never met Joanne again.

27

Nor All Thy Tears

I had been at the restaurant for seven months, and from what I overheard the management were pleased with me.

An urge to speak to my mother became impossible to suppress. It had been too long since I had heard her voice. I thought briefly of telling her that I had finally beaten my disease through sheer willpower, that Joanne Burton was in love with me, but shrank from the lie. Under the influence I couldn't begin to separate truth from fantasy but, when sober, I had no desire to bend the rules – even slightly. I hesitated yet again and then decided I had to phone and, if pressed, I would say my abstinence was brief and say nothing of love.

Dad's voice seemed a thousand miles away and I faltered, 'C-c-could I speak to my mother, please?' It was as if I were speaking to a stranger.

The long silence that followed made me even more nervous, then he spoke. 'Your mother loved you more than life itself, and she was so devastated by what you had become, she walked in front of a car and ended her life.'

Something was gripping my throat and choking the life out

of me. I struggled to breathe; a dizzy feeling swept through my head aggravating the nausea in my throat. My father was still talking – I had missed it all – but his voice droned on about inquests and funerals.

'Hello, hello, are you still there?'

'Yes, I'm here,' I said slowly. 'I'll come up at once.' And then, almost as an afterthought, 'If you don't mind.'

'When you come I'll show you the grave, but you can't stay here.' He was not unfriendly, simply firm.

'Are you all right, Nick?' The friendly voice belonged to the hall porter. I did not answer, but rushed past him out on to the street. At full speed I ran to Leicester Square and on towards Piccadilly. I was at the Haymarket before I stopped, sweating profusely and gasping for breath. I wanted desperately to speak to Joanne but I did not have her telephone number because, of course, our relationship was flawed.

My head was full of noises and I was swaying on the spot. Grasping hold of the railings, I coughed up the phlegm in my throat. The good times ... it was always the good times you remembered when someone died; but Christ! when it's your own mother ... My face was soaked in sweat and I dropped my head on to my arms which were supported by the railings and wept. Then, slowly and deliberately, I retraced my steps back to Leicester Square and went into the nearest bar.

'Pint of bitter and a large brandy please.' My voice sounded unbelievably shaky and I could see from the expression on the barman's face that it showed.

'You all right, sir?'

I nodded. The glass felt so alien in my clammy hand that it might have been years since I had last raised one to my lips. I had three more brandies, a further pint and then returned to my room at the club. Lying awake all night, I fell asleep in the early hours of daylight. At 11am I dressed and, before leaving, I had the foresight to leave a note for the catering manager stating I was taking a few days off due to family bereavement; then I went to my building society in Moorgate and withdrew fifty pounds.

On the Birmingham train from London I settled down with half a dozen cans of beer. I then patronised the buffet-car for further supplies and was well oiled by the time the train drew into Birmingham's New Street Station. I hired a car and, arriving at the village where my father lived, earlier than intended, I decided to drive on to a quiet spot and sleep it off. As I parked the car, the years rolled away and a teenage girl-friend was by my side. My band had a booking that night and we were sitting, relaxing, watching the swans on the river bank in the sunshine ... I slept and slept ...

It was dark when I awoke and I realised that my father must be waiting for me. Having written me off as totally unreliable, he probably thought I was lying drunk somewhere ... I shuddered, brushed myself down and combed my hair in the car's wing mirror.

Driving back through the village towards my old home, I noticed as I passed the church clock, it was only just after 9pm. I would explain away the delay as a traffic hold-up on the motorway and pulled into the driveway.

Father opened the door and I followed him into the kitchen where I had happily practised a thousand songs with my guitar. My sister immediately started hurling obscenities at me from an adjoining room where she was sitting with her fiancé. No doubt she had every right ... Seeing there was only going to be aggravation I suggested to Father we went for a drink and, after some persuasion, he agreed. We visited a few of my old haunts, but it was a painful experience. First I tried a soft drink and then a bottle of beer but I had no stomach for the stuff. I ached for my sobriety and the respectable way of life I had known and enjoyed at the restaurant.

Father was his quiet, reasonable self and he seemed to be encouraged as I told him of my attempts to rehabilitate myself. Naturally the mood was sad, and there were long silences when neither of us knew what to say.

The conversation revolved around anything and nothing and then, inevitably, 'How exactly did she die?'

He unfolded his arms and leaned heavily on the saloon-bar

table, gazing at the floor. 'She was hit by a car on a straight piece of road. No one knows officially why ...'

There was another long silence and I felt a huge lump in my throat and tears welling in my eyes. 'Did she suffer?' I choked.

'No, she was killed instantly,' was the toneless reply. 'Her mind had been deteriorating for some time, which is why we did not sue the driver ...' He paused again, then continued: 'She had a terrific amount of worry to put up with.'

The statement stabbed like a knife. 'You mean me?' I said emptily.

'Well, mothers love their children, but your mother's adoration of you was beyond description. She idolised you, you were her life. You were somebody to be proud of for so long and then the downhill road ... the terrible fall from grace.' I was too full to say anything. I knew, only too well, that what he was saying was true.

'We know of at least a dozen occasions when you came home and did the rounds of people who knew you as a normal person, and borrowed money with fantastic and preposterous stories. Every time your mother went down the road someone would stop her and she would feel obliged to pay them something and they would say, "Whatever's happened to Nick? He used to be such a nice boy." It would break her heart, she would come home and cry for hours. God almighty! Your sister and I hated you – and with good reason.' His hands gripped the table, knuckles showing white, and I wondered if he would ever be able to forgive.

'What can I say?' I hung my head. 'I can't put things right now.'

He looked at me, pity in his eyes, and said, 'No, not now you can't; it's too late for that ... '

We left the pub and drove to an hotel in silence. They had vacancies and I booked a single room for two nights. We parted in the foyer, with Father reminding me that he'd ring in the morning and show me the grave. I lay awake throughout the night and must have looked awful when I entered the breakfast room. I could only manage a coffee, I badly needed a drink.

When I left the hotel, I remembered a pub that opened at ten; but it was still only eight-thirty. Desperate, with all my good intentions cast aside, I drove around for a time – shaking a little and perspiring freely from the effects of withdrawal, then I spotted a licensed grocer's sign over a shop. These were the days when they would not sell alcohol out of official licensing hours.

'Sorry, sir, we do not sell alcohol before eleven.' The manager, in his white coat, was a formidable sight but I was undeterred.

'I realise that, but Mrs Simpson has had one of her attacks and the nurse sent me out to get some brandy. What do you recommend?'

The man visibly relaxed and selected a half-bottle.

'I don't think I know the lady so I shall have to take you at your word,' he said, as I paid. 'Anyway, give her my best wishes.'

I left hurriedly, no longer able to control the trembling. It took me over thirty minutes to find a deserted place but the symptoms were eased, simply by being sure of the brandy's presence. I parked the car, locked it carefully and walked towards some nearby woodland. Sitting down against a fallen tree-trunk, I broke the seal and drank a grateful toast to Mrs Simpson. The liquid burned like fire and, by the time the bottle was finished, everything in the world was beautiful. My mother was alive and I was a star ... I closed my eyes.

The sound of a nearby tractor being started brought me back to grim reality, the terrible mess I had made of my life. Retracing my steps I drove to an early-opening pub and settled down with a beer and the morning paper. Only then did I remember that my father was going to ring the hotel. Hurriedly finishing my beer, I set out to find a telephone. We arranged to meet an hour later.

The churchyard had many memories for me, my afternoons at the Sunday school and the years I had spent in the choir. There was the privet hedge that all 'new boys' were thrown into upon initiation, and we had already passed many familiar gravestones after walking through the lichgate. Mother had been buried near an evergreen tree, close by the door to the vicar's vestry, at the rear of the church.

'There's not much to see at the moment but eventually we shall have a stone.' These were my father's first words since we arrived.

It had always been an open, grassed area where in summer the choirboys had romped around while awaiting the start of Evensong. I must have run around many a time, enjoying the sunshine, over the very spot. Again I heard the vicar's voice chastising me for getting grass stains on my white surplice ...

'We had talked of cremation.' Father's voice broke the spell, ' ... but I knew that mother really favoured burial,' he added, almost as an afterthought.

'I'm glad, Dad,' I whispered.

He turned and looked at me. 'It's a long time since you called me that, son.'

'Yes, I know,' I murmured. 'Everything's a long time.'

We walked slowly back to the lichgate and Dad offered me his hand. 'Go and do your best. I shall think of you.'

With tears streaming down my face I took his outstretched hand; then he turned away and I was alone.

I walked up the path and entered the church. An old photograph hung on the wall inside that beautiful building and my face, eighteen years younger, stared back at me, smiling. All the old choirboys were there. I was standing next to David. He had written a story about me for the local paper when I had appeared in court for deception. Stephen, a television producer. Martin, now a lecturer at a university. Keith, a schoolteacher. And myself – an alcoholic. I walked back to my mother's grave and looked down at the simple plot that held all that was left of her. I sank to my knees beside the grave and parted the grass with my fingers as though it was her hair and, solemnly, I made a vow. 'I'm going back to London now, Mum; but I swear I'll make it – for you.'

Rising to my feet I felt a light rain against my face and, pausing only for a brief moment, I turned and walked away –

an alcoholic who had made a promise. The rain was heavier now and, from the shelter of the lichgate, I scanned the skies. My lips were pressed tightly together as I shook my head; there was no rainbow messenger soaring across the heavens ...

'It's all up to you, Nick!' I said, and sprinted for the car.

28

Downward Spiral

I considered my predicament from every angle, but, on my arrival in London, I was still undecided as to my next move.

I walked around the crowded streets looking at various shop windows and sniffing hungrily at the different food aromas that wafted from countless eating-houses. No matter what time of day, Earl's Court is always milling with people, and soon I was tired of being jostled and walked straight into a pub without thinking.

'Yes, sir?' The barman's voice caught me by surprise and I ordered a pint of bitter – more through embarrassment than anything else. It lay on the counter for a moment or two, and then it was in my hand and I was drinking the liquid greedily. An hour later I was drunk and awoke the next morning in an hotel bed. I had no idea how I managed to get it and I didn't care. All I craved now was another drink as I was suffering from an almighty hangover. I got to the Tube station and went through to the Monument.

Before eight o'clock I was seated, with other familiar faces, in the early-opening pub opposite the fish market. I was back to my old way of life. Three days later I had lost my clothes, spent my money and was standing, dejectedly, with four other alcoholics by the fire at Spitalfields.

The months that followed are a jumbled mass of hazy twilight memories, some amusing, all of them painful and none to be recommended. I drank whatever I could get my hands on to relieve the ghastly withdrawal pains, and I squirm at the memory of some of the concoctions that passed through my body. Meths, aftershave, hair lacquer, rendered down boot polish and metal polish. Others I could identify more by effect than by taste and, for good measure, cough medicine containing alcohol!

One of my fellow down-and-outs had stolen this mixture from a chemist and it was certainly potent. As a bonus, we had the satisfaction of knowing it was not doing as much damage as the other stuff, and it helped us sleep as well. But it led to my appearance at a magistrates' court with two elderly Irishmen.

I knew them only as Tipperary and Corky, and we were charged with stealing. As best as I can remember, an old friend of Corky's had offered us the mixture for fifty pence the previous afternoon. One of our number had just received his Social Security handout and had paid up, so we all trooped off to collect the medicine. Apparently it had originally been in bottles, and the friend had emptied them all into a large polythene drum – also stolen from the chemist! We managed to get it back to our fire, and were singing merrily when the police arrived.

The next thing I remember clearly was waking up in a police cell. I was aware that I was in a filthy state – having slept rough for a long time – but you become conditioned not to notice just how filthy you've become if your surroundings are the same. The cell was very basic, but it was clean, and I was dismayed by my appearance and the way I smelled.

Tipperary, Corky and I were driven to court in a van. Before this we had been ordered to wash in a manner that brooked no argument. We sat in the waiting room with other men and women and, after a short time, a lady usher came in and read out case numbers and the names of the defendants that corresponded with them. Then, to my surprise, she announced, 'Murphy, O'Grady and Price'. Tipperary and Corky answered to the first two, and then I felt a dig in the ribs. Instinctively I sensed that Price must have been invented in the stupor of the previous night, which was now blotted out for ever by alcohol. As confidently as I could I answered, 'Yes, I'm here.'

'You three are next,' she said, and walked smartly away.

As soon as she had gone and we were alone, I nudged Corky and asked him, 'Is that the name I gave?'

He said nothing, but nodded, and I began to wonder if I could get away with the deception.

We were called soon after, and each of us pleaded guilty to the charge. The chairman of the magistrates scratched his head and regarded us with a baffled look on his face. Then he spoke.

'What on earth possessed you to steal cough medicine?'

For some reason he had singled out Corky as our spokesman and directed the question at him. Now Corky was a man of few words at the best of times, and this was certainly not one of his best. He gazed into space, shifting uncomfortably from one foot to the other as the chairman waited for a reply. Seconds passed in an embarrassing silence and then the chairman spoke again.

'Well, are you going to answer? What good did it do you?'

Suddenly Corky's face changed. It was as if he had seen the light; as if all life's mystery had been swept away and he could see the object of it all. Gazing up at the magistrate, he spoke up clearly.

'Well, soirr, I've never had a cough since!'

The court erupted and even the banging of the gavel on the bench seemed muffled.

'Order! Order!' shouted the chairman and, when order was restored, 'case adjourned for further reports.'

We were taken out and, eventually, introduced to a probation officer who told us that we would have to book into a hostel and report to him each day. At this point we were separated and I never saw the other two again, but the probation officer, took me by car to a reception centre run by the Social Services. I was made to take a bath and my clothes were taken away to be cleaned. Then I was given a bed in a large dormitory, with about a dozen other occupants. That night, for the first time in about two months, I slept in a proper bed.

A number of things remained unexplained, like the reason I had given the wrong name and, somehow, managed to get away with it, but I decided the London courts must be filled with dossers, sent up for petty crimes, who were more of a nuisance than anything else. The courts had to take some action but, since little or no sense could be expected or extracted from a wino, we were usually dismissed as hopeless cases. As for myself, by the end of the week I was again sleeping rough and never heard about the matter again.

In the months that followed I was arrested many times for 'vagrancy' and being 'drunk and disorderly'. Time and time again I managed to talk my way out of trouble by saying I was an alcoholic and just about to be dried-out with the help of a friend. I used a variety of aliases and was usually released. These events are all very hazy in my memory, but I was lucky to stay out of society's correctional clutches.

But now I had become more pathetic than ever, never washing and drinking all the alcoholic rubbish in God's creation. One day I stumbled against some building materials that were being used for repairs at Liverpool Street mainline station. Sheets of wood had been left, leaning against a wall, exactly opposite the staff tea-room. They were about eight feet by five and, as there was ample room to crawl behind them, I used to sleep there at night.

The small hidden area was warm, and I would sneak in as early as six o'clock some nights. In time I became aware when the staff came and went off duty. Quite a few of them brought sandwich tins, and I had plenty of time to help myself. I was crafty, and only took one item from each tin. Later, lying snug and hidden, I overheard some amusing comments.

'Do you know, George, I'm sure our Ethel packed me an apple.'

141

'That's two bloody nights running the wife has forgot me Mars bar!'

'Fred! have you bin drinkin' my coffee?'

I know for a fact that they began to suspect one of their own number, but I was never discovered.

Then the inevitable happened. One evening I arrived and the boards were gone and, with them my sleeping-place.

More and more I began to follow my fellow drop-outs to the soup kitchens and hand-out places. There I would eat a little, collect a few pence and buy anything with an alcoholic content that was going cheap. Every day I begged in the streets and slept wherever I could. I was beginning to feel very ill, my stomach ached almost continually and my eyesight was also affected. Deep down I knew I was dying. If something in the way of a miracle didn't happen soon, I knew it was only a matter of time.

One morning, sitting on the steps of St Martin in the Fields, I suddenly decided to leave London. I had an overwhelming desire to escape all the loneliness and hopelessness. If I was going to die, I wanted to die away from this place where I was nothing but an embarrassing statistic to some local government department. I was feeling terribly weak, but I formed a plan and it only needed a little luck to succeed.

Two hours later I was at the dreaded Scarborough Street. There were a few familiar faces about – no names – just men I had seen many times before, and two I remembered in part-icular. One was a youngster, about seventeen or eighteen, and the other was a man in his fifties. The only chair still vacant in the room, was between them.

I hesitated, the old man was suffering from a particularly nasty type of cancer. He had a hole in his cheek where the disease had eaten the flesh away, a large piece of sticking-plaster was all that concealed his molars. The disease was gradually working its way to the corner of his mouth, and the stench of rotting flesh was the poor man's constant companion. He lived in the hostel in Petticoat Lane and, many times in the past, the smell had ruined my appetite. I felt tremendous sympathy for him but, to be near him was almost intolerable. However, on this occasion, the circumstances were different and I sat down between them.

The young man was the silent type and a little retarded. Despite my weak condition, and his lack of conversation, I attempted to interest him in several topics so that I could face away from the unfortunate man next to me.

I was thankful when the older man was called for interview and, soon after, it was my own turn. I was so weak that it was with great difficulty that I managed to get over to the booth to which I had been summoned on the intercom.

The plan I had formulated was simple, all I needed was a sympathetic ear. My luck was in. I told the interviewing officer that I would never be able to improve my standard of living as long as I received bed-tickets and the usual small amount of money. I asked if I could have some extra cash in order to get a small bedsit and make a break from community hostels, as I was rapidly becoming institutionalised. I signed my form and she told me to take a seat.

I expected nothing more than my usual seven tickets and a few bob pocket-money. An hour later I was still contemplating my fate. I became very restless and felt worse than ever. Just as I was about to return to the counter to query the delay, my name was read out with half a dozen others. I found myself at the end of the queue at the paying-out booth and tried desperately to contain my impatience. After showing my identification, I signed next to the amount column in the book, ignored the total, slipped the envelope into my pocket and hurried out, as best I could, into the fresh air.

After walking a few yards, a voice hailed me and the young man I had been talking to joined me a little breathlessly.

'Can I buy you a drink?'

He seemed so anxious to please that I smiled and nodded. From then on he amazed me by chatting continuously as we walked towards Houndsditch Post Office – the ritual place for cheque-cashing.

We were in Middlesex Street at the Aldgate end by the large

P&O shipping office when I ripped open the envelope containing my cheque, I stopped dead in my tracks. Thirty-nine pounds! To me it was like a cheque from Littlewoods, the amount was equal to two weeks' average national wages at the time and I was over the moon. I decided to spend some of it on real booze, contrary to any plans I might have originally entertained.

My young friend insisted on buying the first round and I savoured the first real non-rubbishy drink for weeks. We chatted idly for some time and I thought that, although he would not be my normal choice of a friend, there was certainly nothing objectionable about him – and who was I to object anyway? In my present state I did not choose friends – I'd just hear a few kind words and tag along ... I had no way of knowing that, two days previously, this young man had committed one of the most violent sadistic murders in modern times. There was nothing to suggest he was anything but a 'bit slow' and out of work. Nevertheless, three days later his face stared out at me from the front page of the morning paper as a murder suspect. He was subsequently found unfit to plead and was ordered to be detained at Her Majesty's pleasure.

My plans for the extra money had been to catch a bus or train away from London and take my chances elsewhere but, with the demon drink, my resolution had quickly evaporated. My general condition had worsened to such a degree that I became drunk on a fraction of the alcoholic intake of a year before. I had pains everywhere. Not just from withdrawal, but others that I was convinced were all caused by the filth that I had been drinking for too long. There had to be something seriously wrong internally. I was getting worse by the hour, and had passed the point where even living or dying mattered ...

If anything good at all came from the extra money received from Scarborough Street, it was that I had retained enough for a bed at the Salvation Army. The following morning I met a former BBC cameraman in the canteen, who had lost his job through drink. He said he had the price of a bottle and would I like to join him? I was penniless again and agreed.

29

Destiny
Part One

I awoke suddenly in a place unfamiliar, a weight holding me down making it impossible to move. Painfully I opened my eyes. An enormous fat slob of a man, bearing an expression best described as evil incarnate, was straddled across me holding a fourteen inch blade across my throat. He spoke through gritted teeth, globules of spit and froth running down his chin and dripping on to my face and neck.

'If you're not out of this flat in three minutes, I'm going to cut off your fucking head and throw it in the river.' I believed him.

I was still dragging on my trousers as I half-scrambled, half-fell down the stairs and once on to the street sank to the ground completely exhausted.

I had no memories beyond my share of the cameraman's bottle, just a blank that was as void and as infinite as outer space. I found fifty pence' worth of change in my pocket, and collecting myself together stood apprehensively at the back of a small queue of people at a bus stop. The eventual arrival would carry me back to the city, as inevitably as a pin to a magnet.

I stood on Lambeth Bridge gazing down at the black swirling waters below and wished I had the courage to jump. I recall putting one foot on the lower wall of the parapet with the intention of hoisting the other one up alongside, this at least would enable me to lean over and make a symbolic attempt. Perhaps some gorgeous blonde or redhead would rush forward to save me. More likely there were a few who would have gladly given me a push; it didn't matter anyway, my body could not find the strength.

I thought back to Joanne and my precious months off the booze that were my longest ever. The magical moments I had spent with her, the satisfaction of the job, those little things that normal people just take for granted.

As I stood contemplating suicide, suddenly and inexplicably I recalled meeting, with Danny, the manager of a pub one night at Oscars. He'd said: 'If ever you want a job, call me.' As I stood on the bridge the pub was less than half a mile away. Slowly, I walked towards it.

I had no idea what I was going to say or how I was going to present myself and a brief glance at my appearance confirmed it left a lot to be desired. I walked off the bridge into Horseferry Road and glanced instinctively to my right as I came to Dean Bradley Street. My attention was attracted by the manager opening the doors of a public house called the Marquis of Granby. I paused for a moment fingering the coins I had left over from the bus fare, just enough for half a pint. I needed courage to go and ask for a job, but the beer I ordered was an attempt to rid me of the anxiety, sweating and the shakes. For a short time anyway.

The manager was not good in the morning, his hand shook slightly as he pulled the half pint and he spilled some of it. Probably to avoid altercation he made a token pull of the pump into a second glass and put it down hard next to the first one. I made an effort to smile, more to myself for my gain than to him for his gift. The beer must have been the first out of the barrel, full of bits, murky, a normal punter would have complained. A serious alcoholic would knock it back without a second thought – I left a drop in the bottom for a reason of my own.

The gents' toilet was archaic. These were the days when health and hygiene were not of today's standards, or if they were no one gave a damn. It had a cell-like window full of cobwebs, spent cigarette ends, a comb with about six teeth and an empty fag packet. The sink in the corner lacked a plug or soap, I didn't even bother to look for a towel. It did have a mirror, I was glad of that, but hardly recognised the man in the glass. I did my best to clean myself up. The water was as cold as ice, I rubbed some into my hair and, picking up the filthy comb, used the few remaining teeth to comb it straight; I ignored the filth.

I returned to my table and the beer left in the bottom of the glass. I remained on my feet facing a window through which filtered a watery sun, the extra light confirmed the rubbish in the glass, matching perfectly my quality of life.

I looked at it closely, swishing it around the glass, then threw it quickly down my throat – I looked up at the clock, it was eleven-thirty a.m. on Monday, 13 December 1976.

I placed the glass on the bar counter next to a pile of serviettes and taking one, turned and walked away. Once outside I stopped to wet the tissue in water in the gutter and used it in an attempt to smarten up my shoes.

The Barley Mow was my destination, a two-hundred-yard walk and situated near Horseferry Road Magistrates' Court, venue for many of my personal appearances. I was barely at the door when a breathless manager burst out on to the street seeking fresh air.

'Good grief!' he exclaimed with genuine pleasure and surprise. 'There's a God after all.'

The last time I had heard that expression was when my father won an autumn double in 1948. Sterope won the Cambridgeshire Handicap and Sportsmaster the Manchester November Handicap and Dad picked up twelve hundred pounds, or as near as damn it.

'For the sake of my sanity, get behind that bloody bar and sack those silly fuckin' barmaids. Wobblin' around on six-inch heels and two-inch skirts and washin' up in bleedin' rubber gloves and customers fifteen deep. I've only been away for a week and the bloody gaffer's gone back to his childhood.'

Bob wasn't a bad bloke, ran a good bar and it needed a lot of skill to keep the Barley Mow going. It was one of the busiest lunchtime pubs in the city of London and it needed the best staff available to cope. For sure, it did not need to rely on dolly birds to pull the trade and I walked into a nightmare. It was not just because the staff were useless, some of it was because I felt so ill and in my condition I would have been hospitalised by modern day standards. I was suffering one long panic attack of anxiety and fear, medically accepted symptoms of alcohol withdrawal, and the shirt on my back was soaked.

'You look like death,' Bob commented.

'I've just got back from burying my mum,' I half lied. 'Got back into London late last night and couldn't get a bed – slept in Green Park on a bench.'

Bob grabbed both my arms and looked deep into my eyes. 'Come upstairs, get a shower and change. I'll come back down and cover for you for as long as it takes.'

He asked about my suitcase. I mentioned an imaginary friend. He didn't push it and loaned me some clothes. Somehow I ran his bar.

Suffering chronic alcohol withdrawal and passing drinks to others that my body and mind were screaming for, is totally unimaginable. I'm not even going to try to explain – except I will offer this, I was once in hospital with an old alcoholic who had been tortured by the Japanese while a prisoner of war. He told me alcohol was crueller than the Japs.

I spent most of my first year sober as a barman. Naturally, with time the symptoms receded but it was a hellish way out and not one I would recommend to others.

What alcoholics do to themselves becomes a mechanical process of destruction. We become machines that, although malfunctioning, refuse to come to a halt and for untold millions throughout the ages, only death turns off the ignition. For the fortunate few, a braking system as intangible as the sickness itself goes into operation, and a realisation begins to form that shows the utter futility of it all.

The words of Mario Savio, though directed as an anti-war

message, sum up perfectly the last days of my drinking:

'There is a time when the operation of the machine becomes so odious, makes you so sick at heart, that you can't take part; you can't even tacitly take part, and you've got to put your bodies upon the gears and upon the wheels, upon the levers, upon all the apparatus and you've got to make it stop.'

30

Destiny
Part Two

The previous fourteen years had seen my life degenerate through alcohol, from respectability and standing in my local community, to gutter level and below.

I had now rejoined the human race again; this time however was different, I had joined a rock group. We were rehearsing four nights a week and decided on a male and female to front a five-piece. We failed to find a girl good enough for the very high standards we had set ourselves, so we placed an advert in the London press.

While all this had been happening to me Lesley Roach had also been having problems with alcohol. Not that she drank, it was her parents. They drank and fought and split up and were reunited with terrifying regularity.

Lesley's mother had three preoccupations in life: her husband, alcohol and her daughter's career. The worse the marriage grew, the more she drank, but nothing could distract her from making her daughter a star.

She enrolled Lesley at a stage school when she was five years old and saw to it that she attended auditions for commercials, films and anything else that was going. Lesley did well. She worked with Robert Shaw, Oliver Reed, Vanessa Redgrave, Bob Hoskins, Edward Fox and Anthony Newley – featured in Alan

Parker's *Melody* and appeared on the West End Stage in the *Good Old Bad Old Days* and *Tom Brown's Schooldays* – she lost count of the television commercials.

One day Lesley and her mother returned home to discover that the house was empty. Not a stick of furniture, not one of Lesley's expensive toys remained. They wandered in a daze through echoing rooms, then Lesley's father arrived.

'We're moving,' he said.

That night they arrived at a small house in Oxford.

'Our new home,' said her father.

He stayed less than two months. On Christmas Day, shortly after they'd opened their presents, he said he had to call in at work.

'I'll be back this evening in time for dinner,' he said.

They didn't see him again for months.

It was always like that. Sometimes Lesley felt as if she lived on a roller-coaster. When Dad returned Mother was happy. When he went away she was desperate. She cried, moped and moved from room to room with a bottle in one hand and a glass in the other.

Lesley worked hard at school and the other children seemed to like her. Sometimes they invited her to their homes for tea; it was then that she realised she was different from other kids. Other children seemed to live in clean bright houses, with clean bright mothers and they didn't have to go to the off-licence several times a day.

She soon realised that she couldn't have friends back to her house without embarrassment. As she grew older she used her theatrical skills with wigs and make-up to disguise herself before going to the off-licence in order not to be recognised. Deep down she knew it fooled no one.

She appeared in *Morecambe and Wise*, *The Cilla Black Show*, *Dixon of Dock Green*, *Folly Foot*. Wasn't Lesley doing well? Everyone said so. Lesley smiled then hurried home to find that her mother had slashed her wrists, blood everywhere – just another day. Father didn't live with them any more. Lesley wouldn't have minded except that he kept coming back and upsetting her mother. Sometimes they fought, sometimes they fell into each others' arms. It was worse when they fell into each others' arms. Her mother had three miscarriages as a result and each one left her more depressed than before.

Despite her drinking, she still found time to follow Lesley's career. She accompanied her to film sets and sat in the audience when she was on stage. Once when Lesley dried up in mid-song and her mother stood up and finished the song for her Lesley thought she'd die of embarrassment. One day when she was eighteen, Lesley's father called round yet again and this time she couldn't control her anger. She told him what she thought of him. That she hated him so much she no longer wanted to bear his name. She was going to choose a new stage-name for herself, so that she could blot him out of her mind for ever. Her father cried, Lesley didn't care.

Not long afterwards Lesley Roach became Kelly Miller.

One day Kelly came home and found her mother suffering from a painful bout of indigestion. She gave her milk of magnesia, alka seltzer, every remedy she could think of but the next day she was still ill. Her mother protested angrily but Kelly fetched the doctor. He explained that she'd had a heart attack.

A few days later while Kelly was working on a commercial for Clarke's Shoes, her mother died.

For a long time she didn't know what to do. She had devoted her whole life to pleasing her mother and now she was gone. Then one day her agent, June Collins, mother of rock star Phil Collins, saw an advert in the evening paper. A rock group was looking for a female vocalist. Kelly had never worked in a group before. It would be a change, she thought, so she went along to the audition ... and met Nick Charles.

Kelly tells me that the moment we met she knew that we would end up together and as we got to know each other we discovered a number of extraordinary coincidences.

We had both been aboard the doomed cruise liner, the *Lakonia,* shortly before it was destroyed by fire. As a down-and-out I had wandered the streets where Kelly had played as a schoolgirl. A song she recorded as a child with disc jockey Ed Stewart, 'Soldier Soldier', was my daughter's favourite song and whenever I heard it on the hostel radio it reminded me painfully of home. On one occasion I stumbled into a cinema to sleep off a hangover and found myself watching one of Kelly's films. Later, slumped in the Salvation Army Hostel with no money to go out, I saw an episode of *New Faces*. The only performer who made an impression was Kelly Miller. Finally, just months before we met, we both lost our mothers, Kelly in September 1975, mine in December the same year.

Many people wonder why Kelly, with her experience of alcoholics, should want to spend her life with one. She and I see it differently. We believe we were destined to meet and marry. Kelly feels that her past experience makes her the ideal partner for me because she understands the problems of alcoholism. For my part, I, with my drinking days firmly behind me, feel my past experience makes me the ideal partner for Kelly because I understand the traumas of her life.

Of course, the newspaper advertisement to which Kelly had replied was to fill a vacancy as a singer in my group, but wherever we worked we were advised to leave the band, form a double act and go it alone. Informing the other members of our decision to do so was not going to be easy, but it had to be done and we planned it for a Saturday at a South London club. The others took it very well in the circumstances and wished us good fortune except that is, for the lead guitarist. Unfortunately we lodged with his mother and leaving the group meant sacrificing our home – such is human nature.

As we got up to cross the floor and leave the club, not even knowing where we were going to sleep that night, there was an announcement from the compère.

'The winner of tonight's raffle is blue ticket number sixty–two.'

We were halfway across the floor in the beam of a blue and white spotlight, Kelly stopped in her tracks holding the winning ticket in front of me. I took it and looked towards the stage at the compère holding the other half of our ticket in one hand and a large bottle of brandy in the other.

Kelly caught my gaze – I smiled a mischievous smile and rolled the ticket into a ball.

'Put it back in and draw it out again,' I said laughing. I tossed the ball into the middle of the floor, grabbed Kelly's hand and we went out into the night with the applause of the audience ringing in our ears.

31

The *Sunday People*,
Jimmy Greaves and Me

Kelly and I found digs in Hounslow, West London, in December 1977 just before my thirty-third birthday thanks to the help of a college student I had met while I was a barman at the Barley Mow. It only consisted of one room in a semi owned by a family of hard-working Indians, but it was our first home together and a base from which to work.

We both found full-time jobs and saved every penny we could for the musical equipment we would need and the wheels to transport it. It seemed as if it would take for ever, but the great day arrived and with it a surprise package – a small terraced house became available for rent two miles away. The day we moved in was quite bizarre. We got the keys at 11a.m. the musical equipment arrived at midday and a second-hand Alfa Romeo arrived mid-afternoon.

Many hours of rehearsals followed as we put our comedy double act together, but one experience will live with me until the end of my days – my first cabaret appearance stone-cold sober.

I suffered acute nausea for a month in the run-up and vomited almost as often as when I was drinking. Two days before, I shook and sweated so badly Kelly wanted to call a doctor. I was reluctant, no medical man could solve this one, it was a battle between me, my soul and the devil fighting to find a way in.

Somehow I overcame the demons without reaching for a drink and the elation of the achievement overcame my poor performance. As an act we started none too well. Individually we were both good quality entertainers, but this 'double act' stuff proved tough. We started on the club circuit almost at once but it was hard going and for a long time we were only mediocre.

Slowly but surely we improved and one night at a club in Hendon we were offered a tour of the northern clubs. They were legendary of course and not for their hospitality, yet in an odd way it was more with excitement than trepidation that we joined the M1 at Brent Cross to perform six shows in Middlesbrough.

The first night we were on with a comedian, Vince Earl, now best known as Ron Dixon in the soap, *Brookside*. The second night with Solomon King who had an enormous hit with *She Wears My Ring* in the sixties, and before the last show on Saturday night we had worked with four of the principal players from the *Comedians* television production, also the cheeky Roy 'Chubby' Brown.

We drove home through the night with just one stop and slept in late on Sunday – I decided that in terms of success we had broken even on the tour, won two, lost two and two drawn. Disturbingly for me, the Sunday papers produced a sad reminder of days not too long ago. The *Sunday People* newspaper reporter Frank Thorne had written an exposé on former international footballer Jimmy Greaves – Jimmy was an alcoholic.

His story was all over the headlines and the nation read it with a deep sadness. We had idolised him as a footballer and marvelled at his skills, it was almost inconceivable that he could be alcoholic. After all, alcoholics were tramps and vagrants who lived in parks and drank in the streets, weren't they? There had been a few examples of alcohol problems exposed in the media but Jimmy had broken the mould. Fit, keen of mind and fast of foot – England international, medals galore! What is this alcohol thing? A television documentary was commissioned in an effort to explain to a questioning public.

I had been sober for a year, I knew how hard it would be so I wrote him a letter of support which I thought might help in the months to come. I was invited to take part in the programme.

Bernie Stringle interviewed me on camera and asked me many questions about alcoholism and my own recovery. One question in particular I requested that should he avoid; he asked it anyway.

'Nick, how would you define alcoholism?'

I have no idea where the answer came from, it was completely unrehearsed, but its effects have lived with me until this very day.

'Alcoholism is cancer of the soul. It gets right in there and eats away all that is good, leaving behind only that which is bad and useless.'

There followed a sackful of mail from people all over the country looking for help and advice – my work had begun.

32

The Appearance of Tommy Edwards

One murky late evening in 1978, I was watching television with Kelly when the doorbell rang. Two men stood at my front door.

'You the guy who fixed up Jimmy Greaves?'

It was a question but it was also a statement.

'Well, not really, Jimmy helped himself, I only gave him moral support at the time,' I said truthfully.

'Well, our boss saw you with Jimmy on the box and he wants to see you.'

Most people would have been scared to death by their arrival in the dead of the night, for me it was different. If you have spent as much time as I have, sleeping rough with cut-throats and subsequently running twenty-four hour helplines, listening to rantings and ravings at all hours, there was seemingly little threat from these two well-dressed 'minders'. Anyway, I was intrigued. They were driving a Jaguar which was around ten years old, but in absolutely pristine condition, it even smelled new.

The traffic was light and in no time at all we were on the

outskirts of Hampstead and passing through the gates of a large house.

If the situation had been less serious the following events would have been hilarious. Tommy Edwards, 'lord of the local manor', was sitting up in a four-poster bed looking extremely sorry for himself with a 'Wee Willy Winkie' night-cap sitting on his head and the saddest dog I have ever seen looking sorrowfully up at him.

'E'es always down when I'm ill,' he said, nodding at the dog. 'You look younger on the telly,' he continued in staccato fashion. 'Did you play with Greavsie?'

I looked at him incredulously. 'I'm not a footballer!' I exclaimed, 'we just met through the *Sunday People* newspaper.'

He seemed disappointed and was obviously a big football fan.

'What can I do for you?' I asked, 'or is it that you have the same problem as Jimmy?'

'Yeah! I just can't bloody stop. My business is falling apart and I'm ill all the bloody time. I did see my doctor once, but he's a prat, he was more drunk than I was, silly bleeder.' He shifted himself slightly and a grimace of pain covered a once handsome face. 'I'm scared to death. Look, I don't trust bloody doctors and you looked friendly enough on the telly, and seemed to know what you were talking about.'

I felt he was leading up to something else but I didn't know what. Suddenly, as if he had just found the courage, he pulled back the bedclothes – the bed was full of blood.

'My God!' I couldn't help the exclamation. The whole thing took me by surprise. I had been sober myself for around two years and had helped alcoholics for all of that time, but this was new. This guy was seriously ill and I had the presence of mind to realise that I would not be the first to tell him he needed hospital treatment – now. Aloud I said, 'I'll come with you to the hospital.' There was a long pause.

'Promise you won't leave me.'

'I promise.'

An hour later he was in the operating theatre. During the

waiting time I talked with his minders who introduced me to Tommy's wife, who was a delightful lady in her mid-fifties. They told me all about Tommy. Apparently he made his living from strip joints, sleazy clubs and gambling casinos in and around London. His life was one glorious alcoholic merry-go-round, now it had caught up with him. He had internal bleeding and cirrhosis and was not expected to live. However, live he did, and so incredible was his recovery, he emerged a new man.

Not only did Tommy's life become a revelation, the lives of many people around him were never quite the same again either. He became a regular member of the local Anglican church, a sidesman and financial supporter. He sold his business as soon as he was discharged from hospital and I was actually with him when he introduced himself to the local vicar. The poor man had been begging for cash to have a leak fixed in the church roof – Tommy's words are worth recording.

'Morning Vic, I'm Tommy Edwards, and I'll 'ave a new roof on this place by tea-time next Sunday. Now, what else do you want? Them choirboys looks as if they could do with some new angel costumes and the door's 'anging off its 'inges.'

I left him quietly, my job done, but I heard of his progress through the grapevine. A few things puzzled me though. I'm damned if I know how he got to be a magistrate and I certainly did not expect to see him with a group of Christians carrying an enormous wooden cross down the high street one Good Friday!

He's now retired, still sober and sends me a thank-you card every Christmas – the world is a better place for a sober Tommy Edwards.

33

On and Off the Road

If the Jimmy Greaves documentary and national newspaper coverage heralded the advent of my work, forming a comedy double act with Kelly and working the northern clubs was the master stroke, because the proceeds financed our first day-centres for alcoholics. While the centres followed a rigid regime based on my own recovery, the theories and structures were maintained by a team leader during my absence.

Touring the club circuit was a revelation and the realisation of a lifetime's ambitions and dreams. We played theatres and clubs that were legendary in the vocabularies of generations of entertainers and they were days that heralded the beginning of the fifties and sixties nostalgia revival.

Such was the equality and camaraderie between us on the club circuit that a famous female singer confided in me backstage of a romance she was having with a female politician. *Opportunity Knocks* winner Gerry Monroe complained humorously that his record company had paid up his last contract by returning unsold copies – he said he had a garage full. A delightful and talented man, no one could take away from him his wonderful successes which included 'Sally', 'Cry' and 'My Prayer'. Don Lang was as frantic as ever and the Ivy League was surely one of the most underrated showgroups on the circuit. Michael Barrymore was known to Kelly from a long ago summer season at the Torbay Chalet Hotel and Norman Collier and Lenny Henry made us all laugh till we cried. Alvin Stardust, Karl Denver, countless chart success groups of the sixties followed, and then of course the *crème-de-la-crème* – the Americans. We appeared with the slick Coasters of Charlie Brown and the amazing Gladys Knight and The Pips. If there is a more talented and charming woman in show business then I haven't met her. We thanked God that tradition meant that we went on stage first, I would have hated to have followed her act.

We took part in hundreds of shows and held our heads up high with the best for seven years. Frequently along the way, because of the television exposure, we were asked to advise on alcohol problems, mainly among members of various audiences who came backstage for autographs. There was one exception, however, and he was a rock-and-roll icon. The day he came to see me I was transported back in time to the days of my teens and the wonders that had existed in my imaginings.

I have many memories of my childhood. Practically all are wonderful and full of long, summer, sun-drenched days in the beautiful Worcestershire countryside. In the nineties, un-imaginable innocence which belongs to another time, another age, another world. One such long summer day in the early sixties I was walking along the River Severn towpath with two or three of my friends listening to a certain pop song for the first time: it was called 'Runaway' and the singer-songwriter was Del Shannon. The American influence upon our music was total at the time, and because of their inaccessibility it became an enigma which created a magical, Hollywood-type aura. My home had only had television for a short time and many of my friends were still without. BBC2 was some years away and Independent Television was relatively recent. It was little wonder that people like Elvis Presley, Roy Orbison and Del Shannon appeared unreal, almost as if from another planet. Silk suits, sequins, magenta lighting on flawless white guitars in blonde or polished veneer flashing from out of glossy colour photos – that's the memory, it's strange that practically everything I have seen from that era since has been in black and white.

Such was the possible dynamic rise of performers in those days that a year later I appeared on the same bill as Del Shannon at a London theatre; afterwards we had a drink together in the artistes' bar.

Now, years later, Charles Westover, better known as Del Shannon, sat across an old battered table from me at my first day-centre. He did not look well, nor did he look much like his publicity photos. In those days he had looked tall, rugged, powerfully built and extremely self-confident; today he looked like he needed a drink.

'I've got an illness called "I ain't got it"' he said in his Texas drawl.

I nodded but told him I'd got it, knew it and had dealt with it.

'Show me how,' he said.

I explained to him that his habitual drinking had led him into an abnormal lifestyle dominated by the need for alcohol. Everything he did was governed by its presence and influenced by the degree of his intoxication. He had now reached a stage in his alcohol addiction where he had become a complete slave to a bottle and he would have to completely readjust his life, with or without AA meetings, to the complete exclusion of liquor if he was to survive.

I warned him that initially, the absence of booze would leave an enormous void in his existence that he would have to learn to fill by self-motivation. 'It's your life – your responsibility and you who will ultimately benefit or suffer depending on the results of your efforts ... '

My voice rose in a crescendo of anger and conviction, and as I leaned forward a droplet of sweat fell from my forehead on to the table between us.

'He gave his blood,' he quoted wiping my perspiration with his finger.

'What are you prepared to give?' I asked him.
'Whatever it takes,' he drawled.
And he did.

34

The End of the Beginning

Both Kelly and I loved the life. It was therefore with deep sadness that the businessman that lurked deep within me sensed the depressing reality of the decline of the club circuit. Many top quality acts had gone back to day-time jobs, some were unemployed, others like us were clinging on by the skin of their teeth.

We relied heavily on there being a backing band at each venue we played. Clubs that were economising decreed that to employ a self-contained act cut the cost of employing a resident band – work became harder to come by.

We decided to employ our own backing and through some local amateur entertainers spotted a jewel in an otherwise crown of thorns – she was a very fine keyboard player and former international sportswoman, whose career had been tragically cut short by injury. Teresa Weiler, now a lifelong friend, has told us many times of the shock of moving from life in the slow lane to being hit by hurricane Nick and Kelly!

It was soon obvious that showbusiness was giving us up. In desperation we turned our eyes to agency and management work with Kelly and I full of ideas and Teresa, now living in, organising the business. It was a roller-coaster of twenty-pound notes to excess one day, and an overdraft the next. Meals out, meals in, and sometimes no meals at all!

We had eventually bought our house in Hounslow for £17,000 and due to learning my craft through sober, but not yet rational, eyes, managed to owe £80,000 on it thanks to a smooth tongue, unbelievable enthusiasm and a bank manager who believed in dreams. Had Teresa not been around I suspect we would have drowned in our own euphoria and nearly did, but for the remaining dregs of the poor girl's resistance to irrational optimism.

At one stage we were putting entertainment into fifteen hundred public houses a week in the London area and money rained in like confetti. The trouble was that the office equipment necessary to cope was on a five-year contract. (Who the hell reads the small print?) We all do now.

When we lost the contract the suppliers insisted on their money, and at one hundred thousand pounds in debt, I needed a drink.

Weeks of hell ensued as I watched ten years' sobriety and achievement dissolve before my very eyes – the bank gave me six weeks to clear the debt or they would go for the property in lieu – I stayed sober.

I ran round like a headless chicken for a fortnight – Teresa took a temporary job to keep us, and Kelly stayed to answer a phone that never rang – I still stayed sober.

I took a stab at the film industry – and missed, tried boxing promotion and lost on points, then I met a playwright who came up with the complete answer to all of my problems.

'You must hand your life over to Christ.' I decided there were more nutters among sober people than there were among the drunks, but went to a religious meeting all the same – anyway there was nowhere else to go. I did not buy the God stuff though – when the chips were down you had to fight, it's a jungle out there! I felt a trip back to bedsit land would probably be something Kelly and I could manage – Teresa had her parents at a push. The trouble was, I had a cat. Bedsits don't allow cats – seemed damned unreasonable because he liked his cold cocoa and the central heating, and anyway he nearly died when he was a kitten.

I was rambling now, my thoughts were muddled at best. I would go for a long drive – I can think better when I'm driving. I went round in circles, straight lines, ovals, probably squares and finished up in a car park. In front of me was a church steeple.

'Jesus Christ!' I thought. 'You can't get away from bloody religion.'

'You called.' The voice belonged to a smiling cleric and I realised I had been thinking aloud.

The poster behind him read: 'If you are tired of sin, step inside.'

'Some wag had written underneath, 'If not, ring King's Cross 4712!'

I smiled – he spotted the reason and I spoke. 'I suppose you have to put up with a lot of that.'

He paused for a moment then said, 'A drowning man clutches after a straw, they all come to us in desperation.'

'What do you tell them?' I asked.

'Simple – just hand your life over to Christ.'

My head jerked, he sensed he was hooking a fish.

'I wish I had a pound for every human being I had seen running around like a headless chicken trying to do their will instead of God's,' he said.

I didn't understand and said so.

'Simple,' he said it again – I thought, if only it was.

'You cannot make things happen that are not meant to be,' he continued. 'Hand your life over to Christ and just wait for things to happen.'

I went home, sat down in my favourite chair, picked up the paper and waited!

'We've got ten bloody days to find a hundred thousand pounds or we're up the bloody pictures, and you're sat down reading the paper. What on earth are you proposing to do?' The voice belonged to Teresa.

I stayed inside the newspaper but said simply, 'I've handed my life over to Christ.'

Kelly called the doctor.

Amazingly, the telephone rang three times within a week. Somebody who knew somebody who knew somebody else who knew me had work for a theatrical publicist! Was I a publicist?

'Teresa, what's a publicist?' I became a publicist for three major West End productions on U K tour.

Only a coincidence of course, but it paid enough to satisfy the bank, bought us much needed time and the cat his cold cocoa.

I had survived the most dreadful trauma of my post-drinking life – sober.

35

Chaucer Just Happened

I once met a famous film producer who expressed an interest in making a film of my life story. When I asked him how he became involved in movies he replied, 'It just happened.' I thought, what rubbish! How can you just happen to become a Hollywood film producer, but now I'm not so sure – you see, Chaucer Clinic just happened.

Most alcoholics' natural desire to help others in their immediate post-drinking life wanes slowly but surely as time passes by. For me this was not the case, one distressed soul became two, became four, became ten and so on. Leases on my day-centres were all too short and I finally approached my own family doctor to see if he could offer more permanent accommodation within his surgery complex.

My plan for rehabilitation is based on my own recovery pure and simple. I was a meths-drinking vagrant who lived under viaducts and in condemned property, sleeping the unconscious sleep, fitfully waking every half an hour to fight off scorpions, spiders and rats that were hallucinations. I loved alcohol and its effect throughout the degeneration of my life. In rare moments of lucidity I missed only the warm alcoholic glow and failed to remember the pain, humiliation and degradation – I sat soaked in my own urine and excrement and pined only for another mouthful.

Everyone who is addicted, no matter how badly, can follow my recovery and return to function normally in a society that likes to drink alcohol.

I advocate a treatment schedule in three parts:

Alcohol addicts have to learn to live in a world alcohol-free and to this end my programme begins with a regime of work therapy between 9a.m. and 5p.m. five days a week. The sheer pleasure that is derived out of the daily accomplishments while sober are a revelation and, oh, so self-satisfying. One of the most valuable aspects has to be the process of self-healing which takes place during these working hours. Vitally, this enables the person to acclimatise him or herself ready for the workplace upon discharge.

The permanent removal of alcohol leaves a void. There are anything up to thirty hobbies, pursuits and interests in place at any one time, a little like courses available at any civic centre. Each individual is encouraged to fill their new-found social time with any of these to form the basis upon which to build their new social lives.

I have associated with problem drinkers, drunk and sober, for thirty-seven years and I have never met two the same. Given this I cannot subscribe to one treatment for all – part three, therefore, is reserved for the individual. Whatever your problems are we will move mountains to put them right.

When I had been sober for one month I felt that it was a great achievement. I was without alcohol for a longer period than at any time since leaving college at seventeen years of age, and at the early stages of realisation that sobriety might just offer something more than an alternative to being drunk. More importantly I felt, 'Well, if I can do it anyone can.'

Ten years later I adopted this as the theme at the first Chaucer Clinic and I shall never forget my introduction to working on a psychiatric hospital estate. I had arranged to pick up the keys for my new-found clinic by meeting one of the hospital management outside the main reception. He would be identifiable by wearing a suit and answering to the name of David.

Sure enough, outside reception, stood a man in a slightly ill-fitting suit who gave me a beaming yet vaguely odd smile.

'Good morning, are you David?'

The reply was deep and slightly musical.

'Ye...s!'

I passed a brief pleasantry and got back into the car expecting him to do the same. I was surprised when he did not. Perhaps I should have opened the door for him, maybe protocol was a little old-fashioned in the health authority system. I got back out and opened the passenger door, and immediately he entered. Conversation was difficult but I struggled valiantly.

'Have you worked for the authority long, David?'

'Ye...s!'

He offered me no more and I concentrated on guiding my car over the humps in the road known as sleeping policemen, which were designed to slow down the traffic, thus protecting the many psychiatric patients who wandered freely around.

'I suppose your work is difficult at times with so many sick people about,' I tried again.

'Ye...s!'

We arrived at the old and now empty Chaucer Ward. I was somewhat relieved and got out of the car, expecting him to do the same – he did not.

I walked round to the passenger side of the car and opened the door.

'Would you like to come with me, David?' I asked ever so slightly sarcastically.

'Ye...s!'

We walked up the pathway to the main doors and stood together, both quite still. I looked at him, he looked straight ahead.

'Have you got the keys, David?'

'Ye . . . s!'

'Are you going to open the door?' Now I was irritated.

'Ye . . . s!'

In the background I saw some psychiatric patients out on exercise walking with a nurse. They were all wearing slightly ill-fitting suits! Suddenly the penny dropped, my God! I had picked up a patient.

'David, shall we go back to the car now?'

'Ye . . . s!'

The twenty yards back to my car were the longest of my life, but they were uneventful. I opened the door for him and he sat in without a word. Back over the sleeping policemen and an eternity later I was opening the door for him outside the main reception.

'Goodbye then David, hope you enjoyed the ride.'

'Ye . . . s!'

I slumped gratefully back into the driving seat, my head in my hands, thankful that the experience was over. Suddenly, I remembered the real man I was supposed to be meeting and looked up with a jerk. There stood a man, resplendent in an immaculate-fitting suit . . . David?

I eased myself slowly from the car, keeping my eyes fixed firmly on him. I caught his glance, he smiled, I nodded.

'Are you David ?' I asked hesitantly.

He answered at once. 'Ye . . . s!'

36

Chaucer's First Patient

The Chaucer Ward was not quite as I had expected. The real David was as repulsed by its general condition as I was and after a few minutes we both rushed outside for fresh air. The place reeked of stale urine and excrement and the floor was an inch deep in a mixture of both, plus rainwater from holes in the roof. There was no electricity, no heating and precious little incentive to take further interest in whatever crazy ideas I might have had. As I left I took a last look over my shoulder and saw a human turd on a window ledge.

Nikki de Villiers was a tennis fan who every year sat glued to her television for two weeks in midsummer to watch Wimbledon, that is until June 1989. She had been introduced to me through a friend who was becoming increasingly concerned about the effect drinking was having on her life. She agreed to at least talk to me. However, when I arrived, switched off Wimbledon, removed her glass of cider and sat down, I wasn't sure if she would listen to what I had to say!

That visit changed her for ever. From that moment on she would cease to think only of today and how much alcohol she would need, but more about what would happen tomorrow and onwards, not just for herself but for hundreds of others.

Nothing happened immediately, but by September she finally stopped drinking. First it was a day, then two, then a whole week and then a month. Suddenly there was something to lose; I had decided to take over the premises at the hospital as it was my only option, and open it as a day-centre for alcoholics. The building needed an enormous amount of work, not the least of which was a mammoth clean-up. Nikki had always boasted to me that she was the best cleaner I'd ever find and she spent the next weeks proving it. As the projected Chaucer Clinic began to take shape, and electricity and water supplies were connected, I started to organise the centre so that it could become residential. I talked of finding a clinic manager and I realised Nikki thought there was a very real career prospect.

Reasons for her not to drink increased but as the price grew higher the task got harder. The real world of work, relationships, emotions and everyday living without a drink was often more than she could handle and there were times when I thought she could fight no more. Suddenly, six months into her sobriety, I realised she was contributing a great deal to the running of the clinic, she was in effect the clinic manager – mind you, the pressure got to her – in her early days she resigned at least twice a day!

By the time I met her she had accumulated a great many problems in addition to her alcoholism. She weighed barely six stone and was anorexic, had survived a disrupted, unstable and unhappy childhood which, without the anaesthetic of alcohol were memories she found terribly hard to live with. All this had to be addressed. Although I offered her ongoing counselling and the benefit of my experiences, I thought I would at least let her visit Alcoholics Anonymous. I consulted Kelly, who was very fond of this new kid on the block, and she agreed that it could do no harm. Nikki hated it.

Many times during the years I struggled to overcome my own alcoholism I was told Alcoholics Anonymous was the only way. I failed miserably at AA. I have no criticism of their philosophy as it was originally written – it was simply not for me, so I did not argue with her reluctance.

Alcoholics are fundamentally angry people. We are angry because we want to be able to drink, but the medical profession and know-alls of the world are telling us we cannot – while holding a glass in their hands. The overwhelming evidence of our experiences of trying to beat the bottle agrees with their thinking, yet instead of accepting the reality we just become angrier.

I steadfastly refused to accept that I had to sit in AA rooms several times a week for the rest of my life, listening to tales of drunken behaviour, however amusing folk made them sound, in order to stay sober. I did try, but became conscious that it often resulted in a competition of who had sunk the lowest or who was the funniest. I became positively fed up with hearing one story from many different people who all stated that they knew they had reached their rock bottom when a dog cocked its leg and peed on them as they lay in the gutter. I construed that, like the comic on the circuit who had his act plundered by other would-be comics, this was a tale worth nicking because it always got a good laugh. Either that or there is a poor canine creature wandering around the City of London doing little other than pissing on drunks. This being the case I think the RSPCA should get there hotfoot before it picks up something that will do it permanent harm and get the poor alcoholic dosser a further bad name! The national tabloid press is forever publishing stories of alcoholic celebrities saved by the magic of twelve steps – I am truly delighted for them, but I attended such a gathering recently where the chairman was the compère and the rest of the acts followed like *Sunday Night at the London Palladium*. Sorry, but while I think abstinence should not be a sad step, neither do I think that it is a game.

When formulated Alcoholics Anonymous was rooted in Christianity with God or Jesus Christ the Higher Power. I believe any watering down of this philosophical doctrine is hypocrisy of the highest degree. I have heard non-Christians told they can choose whatever they wish as their higher power, varying from the sublime to the ridiculous. While I can easily accept other religions choosing their Gods as figureheads, anything less is not only sacrilegious, but an insult to two very genuinely committted men who wrote the rules of the fellowship. Anyone considering AA who is not committed to a God is almost guaranteed to fail and no amount of 'bending the rules' to accommodate for numbers can be a substitute.

Finally, on this controversial issue I have a personal bone of contention. Alcoholics have to rejoin the human race in a society that has very little sympathy for them. For good quality sobriety they must do this, and forming little private fraternities, as a world within a world, is almost like setting up a kind of leper colony that can only lead to isolation. It can become purgatory and generate a 'them and us' situation which turns the illness into a millstone carried for life.

I think it not coincidental that many mainstream Christian AA twelve-step believers have broken away and formed a Christian-only group called Alcoholics Victorious. I wish them Godspeed.

As alcoholism is a progressive illness, there are many stages along the way where treatment is appropriate. I chose to pitch my own particular brand for those at the end of the road, and Chaucer is affectionately known as the last alcoholic bus stop on the way to the cemetery. Incredibly, it has now turned full circle, with people from all walks of life benefiting from the sharp shock of entering a recovery programme alongside homeless victims. They all have to learn that to treat alcoholism and attain sobriety means a permanent process of unlearning all the arrogance, deceit, conceit, illusion, delusion and dishonesty that, through alcohol, they have been training themselves into for years. It means killing a part of yourself and undergoing a kind of death.

Work therapy is the main theme – many if not all applicants have long since became unemployable and getting back into the habit of clocking-in helps to restore self-esteem, pride in one's capabilities and credibility in the eyes of others.

It is a relatively short working day, containing an hour for lunch, a refreshment break in the morning and again in the afternoon. Everyone takes part and there are twenty ongoing preoccupations. Spare time is filled with many hobbies and pursuits, all designed to form a new social life and fill the time previously spent drinking alcohol. The astonishing number and variation of these has prompted many a visitor to say: 'Gosh! I would enjoy it here, not even Butlin's offers that much.'

The week is punctuated with one-to-one meetings, group get-togethers and an open choice to discuss people's individual problems with whoever they wish among members and staff with varying lengths of sobriety. Everyone on the treatment side at Chaucer is an alcoholic who has recovered through the project.

If I had to sum up the Chaucer theory simply, it would be to say that it is a miniature of life in the community where they learn all the lessons of life without a glass in their hand. They will meet people they love and people they hate, folk to tolerate, some who will cause grief and others who will fall over themselves trying to help. There will be rules not to be broken and time schedules they must keep or be penalised, they must keep themselves clean and their room tidy – wipe your feet, don't get mud on my carpets...

Does it sound familiar? Of course it does! because, it's just like any normal home anywhere in the country!

For the alcoholic it has ceased to be the norm, therefore Chaucer goes back to basics.

There is a group at Chaucer 'for those near and dear' ably run by Kelly. She offers help and advice whenever she can. There are no magic wands, no one-line cures, but there is a process of recovery for them also. The miracles are usually reserved for the alcoholic, for those who suffer for many years in an alcoholic household the recovery is often a long and winding road.

Detoxification for the alcoholic clears away the poison and the anaesthetic effects that continual consumption of the liquid creates. Physically, they seem cured and their reaction is often,

'Well. I'm all right, I've got my act together, what's all the fuss about?' making no allowance for the hell created over many years by excessive drinking habits.

Kelly's group find that, in the vast majority of cases, the loved ones are left just as sick psychologically as the alcoholics, due to living a life of insanity during the drinker's reign of alcoholic terror. It may take several years for the alcoholic's psychological equilibrium to even out – it can take considerably longer for the loved one to completely recover, and for some it may never happen.

Naturally, the Chaucer Clinic programme and its structure did not take place overnight, and I am often asked to relate tales of those early days of transition from a condemned building to the now mightily impressive Chaucer Clinic.

A strange phenomenon had occurred in West London.

Odd bits of wood and discarded, damaged and worn out furniture disappeared from skips at all times of the day and night. Scavenging became an art form developed by deft skills born out of the necessity for somewhere to sit and sleep. Items considered of no value to man or beast would be admired in awe during the weeks and months that followed by onlookers informed that they had been reshaped by the Chaucer restoration department.

'Rubbed down, carpentered, re-upholstered, varnished and stained by alcoholic vagrants,' was the proud cry.

'Nonsense!' was the reply.

'True, as God's my judge,' the honest answer came.

I was as pleased as punch with myself for the instigation – but proud, oh, so proud, of those who had stayed sober long enough to do the work.

Recycling was as popular as refurbishment. Two scaffold poles and an old tent cut up became a stretcher. Four-by-two roof joists became garden furniture and bed-frames. Floorboards became tables, sheets became tablecloths. An old coffin without a lid, fixed sideways on, with a strip-light inside and a signwriter's sober lettering upon perspex, provided Chaucer's first sign over the front door. Wherever there was demolition, useless bits of wood became window frames and the first catering kitchen emerged from God only knows where. The Chaucer Marauders became a local legend – usually in their own lunchtimes. Nothing has changed to this day and I sit in a chair that arrived from the restoration department via a skip in Hammersmith.

We began by renewing the lease on our initial building by telephone every Friday night, then graduated to premises abandoned by the hospital due to a serious fire. Through many traumas, obstacle courses, petty jealousies and insane attempts at character assassination, life went on. We undoubtedly would not have survived without the dedication of a small circle of friends, led by Regional Consultant Psychiatrist Dr David Marjot, trustees Roger Brading and David Ellis, and complete faith in ourselves and our beliefs.

Alcoholism is not a fashionable cause, and although a registered charity I could not run Chaucer for three months on all the donations received for my work in twenty years.

I was so naïve at the outset, that our original building was up and running before I learned of residential allowance. I did so accidentally during a conversation with the Social Security department in Glasgow. It was therefore, with great excitement, that I put in an initial claim for a young woman who had followed closely behind Nikki for treatment. When the cheque arrived for three hundred and sixty-five pounds, there was a party atmosphere as the patient took the cheque to the local Post Office for cashing. Meanwhile at Chaucer we arranged to buy some extra food to celebrate the occasion when she returned. Three weeks later we received a card from Tenerife saying, 'Wish you were here!' From then on the bearer of each payment had a chaperon who would return with the cash.

The next step was to set up an administration department, a task our friend Teresa was well qualified to do, so I invited her to come and see the new clinic.

She arrived one dreadful winter's morning in a beautiful business suit and a magnificent executive motor car and listened patiently as I gushed forth my dreams for the future.

'I'll match your present salary and car and buy you a house if you'll come back and run the administration.'

She had to give notice – tiresome bureaucracy – arrived eventually with her employment papers – I found a plastic bag with receipts in, a Mini that was so old it had more holes than an average colander – hers to borrow two days a week. The first week I managed to pay her twenty pounds.

'I didn't say from day one,' was my lament.

Later. 'I didn't say first month either.'

Teresa set about the task and did what administrators do – they organise – set up systems – sort out the accounts – get things in order.

Fortunately for Chaucer she rose to the daunting and challenging task, and settled for a share in the Mini!

The creation of the administration system was no less impressive or meteoric than that of the rehabilitation programme itself. The two together, with the emergence of a newly decorated interior and beautiful ornamental garden, dramatically impressed an almost never-ending procession of admirers.

I occasionally allow myself the luxury of standing back and looking at the magnitude of the achievement. Not as an ego trip but in sheer wonderment at the knowledge that a motley bunch of social misfits, dismissed by society as unemployable, could have built, literally from the ashes of a fire, a facility that does business with health organisations all over the world.

Patients have been admitted from throughout the United Kingdom and from as far afield as the United States of America, Canada, Japan, the former Yugoslavia, the Philippines, Czechoslovakia, many African countries, Germany, France and Belgium.

That this phenomenon could have risen from a London sewer is stuff that fiction is made of. That Chaucer is not a figment of an over-active imagination is a tribute to many triumphs over much adversity. That it stands as a monument to thousands of dead who have no Cenotaph, or victory over an evil foe to show for their sacrifices, provides tribute enough.

In many respects I am responsible for the humour and constant leg-pulling that is so much part of this now serious and almost sacred icon. The reality is that without the laughter it would not have got beyond first base. I look back and laugh at the rats that fed from my body and encourage others to see their own individual horrors in the vein that it is 'only not funny if you are going to do it again'.

My everlasting memories of detoxification units and rehabilitation projects, both from a patient's point of view and that of a visitor, are like a London smog with an ambience of sadness and misery hanging as thickly as the smoke. I had a friend who was on the cleaning staff at one new hospital, where the detox unit, in a stark contrast to the rest of the facility, was turned into a pigsty.

I was determined that no such conditions would prevail at Chaucer and I would fight apathy on an ongoing basis as the eighth deadly sin.

Nikki meanwhile had made staggering progress, despite having one of the most severe case-histories I had encountered. Now people look at her, General Manager of the largest alcohol unit in the country, and think she must have been blessed with some magical strength. I can assure you she was not. Like me, some of the most wonderful days and events in her life have been in the early sober years but some of the most desperate, black, hopeless and tough days have been in there as well. I believe that what set us apart from alcoholics who still drink (and those who do not have a good quality sobriety) is that we wanted to stop drinking and wanted what sobriety had to offer. We took the opportunity, stuck at it and made a success, achieving in sobriety heights we would never have believed possible in our drinking days.

37

Point of Return

It was a sunny spring morning when we received our licence for our first residential rehabilitation clinic. A mother vixen and her family of four cubs walked by my office window with Jerry, Nikki's ginger cat, bringing up the rear – almost a walk-past in mock salute. I'm convinced that either Jerry thought he was a fox or the vixen assumed he was a cub.

The piece of paper confirming registration heralded the beginning of a new age. It would be necessary to compete in the market place from now on and vital to communicate with health authorities further afield.

It was midsummer when Teresa and I found ourselves at a big health authority in the Midlands and *déjà vu* not for the first time in my life sent a strange shiver down my spine. The sense of *déjà vu* was because I recognised vaguely where we were. There was a massive pub on the corner of a mini crossroads. The small access down the side, barely a lane, was familiar and led to somewhere I knew but could not recall – I took the turning.

Teresa exclaimed her annoyance at my deviation from the instructions she had given me and shook the map irritably. It was a cul-de-sac and a large familiar church barred our way.

'My mother and father were married here.'

'Pardon?'

I realised at once that I was whispering and repeated myself, 'Mum and Dad…they were married here…I was christened. …Granny and Grandad are buried somewhere over there.' I pointed west.

I stopped the car and walked through the churchyard towards the main door of the church – it was locked.

'We're wasting time!' I had forgotten she was there, my mind was racing…

'I came here twenty years ago in another incarnation, at least it seems that way.'

'Can I help you?'

The vicar was a friendly man and was quite interested when I told him my story and how keen I was to locate my signature in the book I had signed. He warned us both that it would be quite a task and once inside the vestry pointed to two stacks of leather-bound visitors' books each ten feet high. Teresa knew my story as well as anyone and was now as fascinated at the prospect as I was, and the vicar left us and we set about our task with a will.

The shadows lengthened, health authorities were temporarily discarded – Mrs P Cameron, New York, USA; Mr and Mrs Jones, Bath, Avon; Jocelyne and Claude Duval, Grenoble, France; Nick Charles, no fixed abode…

'My God, I've got it!' I exclaimed. Teresa looked over my shoulder with a dusty face and blackened hands collected from the age-old volumes.

I sank to the floor, feeling weak, tearful and strangely disorientated – my eyes had not left the page. I was riveted to the words but not to my name or lack of address; there was a place for comments in the final column and it was the words I had written there so long ago, and my many years of sobriety that had caused time to stand still. They said:

'If I return to this place sober and read these words – there will indeed be a God…'

38

The Circle

A patient had arrived at the clinic for assessment from a health authority in the Midlands; Nikki's head appeared around my office door to let me know Teresa would probably be needed because the funding was complicated.

I walked up the corridor and took a quick glance through an inspection window at the man I was to assess for admission. I didn't like surprises. He looked familiar, older than I remembered, but familiar just the same. I racked my brain, scanning what seemed several lifetimes. Perhaps he was one of my father's friends or a former employer or...I suddenly felt light-headed. I was a boy again, it was summertime and I could see the patient as he used to be.

The Black Dog Hotel, situated by the River Severn and the centre of affluence, was the place where all the beautiful people met to show off their gleaming motor cars, latest fashions, gold and diamonds. Sunday morning was a revelation for a motor car-loving eleven year old boy.

Cars came in any colour you liked by the fifties. Blues, greens, yellows, reds, two-tone variations and white-wall tyres were in abundance and seen everywhere.

The long sleek Zephyr Six in two-tone blue and white was the boy's favourite, but he did have a sneaky regard for the yellow and white Ford Consul which was a somewhat poor relation. Hillman had a Minx which deserved a second look, but the Californian simply took his breath away. The chrome on the Vauxhall shone in the sunlight and glittered like precious stones, and the light in the grille of the Wolseley, together with pencil-thin shape was full of romantic innuendo.

The drivers were mainly men and had suits made of expensive cloth and shiny faces that always seemed red and full of laughter. The ladies were exquisitely dressed with long, beautiful wavy hairstyles and summer dresses with full petticoated skirts which bounced in the summer breeze.

The youngster sat in the sunshine strumming a guitar he had been given by his parents for Christmas, occasionally stopping to marvel at a new Jaguar, Daimler or Rolls. One day he would earn a lot of money from his singing and guitar playing and drive a new Zephyr Six in blue and white two-tone carrying a beautiful lady and park it dead centre in the car park, at the Black Dog.

The romance of those summer days receded and shifted to other things, and the little boy did not grow up. The memories were still vivid and names and faces lived on. There had been Herbert Tredegar, head of a business empire, Tim Seymour-Briggs who owned a carpet factory, and the Colonel who had inherited a large estate. There were these and others in the Black Dog when the boy became a client, but he didn't like them now and it did not bother him that he was not accepted.

He passed noisily through alcohol and trial and tribulation. His life became messy and unmanageable. He nearly died at the hands of 'Black Dogs' and red happy faces. Then he changed his lifestyle and views and opened a treatment centre for victims with red unhappy faces, troubled hearts and broken lives. It was too late to help the Colonel, he died from cirrhosis and Seymour-Briggs developed a blood clot as a result of drinking and died in a bar at a 'Black Dog'.

It was Herbert Tredegar sat behind the glass. The Zephyr Six had long gone and so had the immaculate suits – only the red face remained. The smile had changed to a haggard, drawn look and he would not recognise the small boy. He had lost his wife and family through 'Black Dogs' and no one found him a useful contact any more. He had no friends, only a few people who lived in the parks and he had arrived to receive help from a small boy who had now become a man.

It was an incredible coincidence, but it had been that sort of year. The number of alcoholics I had helped was approaching the eight thousand mark and Kelly and I had received an invitation for tea on the lawn at 10 Downing Street with the Prime Minister and his wife. I had advised the Department of Health on the Rough Sleepers Initiative, was meeting with the Football Association on a policy review and Kelly and I had moved to a new house in Surrey. The national press and various agencies were regular callers and I had appeared on TV and radio whenever my input was considered useful...nothing however could have prepared me for 15 November 1996.

The day started badly. Teresa was to undergo a major operation and Kelly, Nikki and I had just telephoned her with a word of encouragement before she went down to theatre.

I heard the post drop on to the hall carpet and the letterbox lid clip back into place. Kelly collected the pile of mail and I heard her footsteps on the stairs, only one for me. The front was printed boldly URGENT PERSONAL PRIME MINISTER. I opened the envelope with trembling hands.

Dear Sir,

The Prime Minister has asked me to inform you, in strict confidence, that he has it in mind, on the occasion of the forthcoming list of New Year's Honours, to submit your name to The Queen with a recommendation that Her Majesty may be graciously pleased to approve that you be appointed a Member of the Order of the British Empire...

Through cascading tears I remembered an evening out with my father and my first ever alcoholic drink when I was seventeen and it had made me sick.

'Don't worry son, it's an acquired taste,' he had said.

I did acquire it and it had taken me on an incredible journey – which was about to lead to Buckingham Palace.

39

Empire Day

The New Year's Honours List was published. Any fears that might have haunted me during the previous weeks that I could somehow have overlooked were dispelled. The girls and I danced a jig and laughed and cried and laughed and cried again. Over a hundred letters and telephone calls followed, the Prime Minister, cabinet ministers, health authorities, doctors, psychiatrists and friends from all over the country, and a Hollywood film director no less. Day after day letters dropped on the mat – Nick Charles MBE – I wondered what the postman must have thought, probably nothing, but I was overwhelmed. Then a buff envelope arrived franked Central Chancery of the Orders of Knighthood, St James's Palace telling me that my investiture would be at Buckingham Palace on 21 March 1997.

It was a beautiful day. I stood in my bedroom and looked out at the garden in wonder that it could be mine. It was exquisitely landscaped by the previous owners and Kelly and I had worked tirelessly to maintain it at somewhere close to the standard they had set. Two robins sat on the patio fence looking up at me inquisitively and a pair of squirrels stopped momentarily to look inquiringly up at my window. I looked back at the garden and tried to imagine the sewer, I tried to imagine the viaduct, I tried to imagine the fire at Spitalfields, I tried to visualise the filth in which alcohol had forced me to live – I could not. I would have to pay one more visit, I must not forget, not even twenty years later, especially not today.

My chauffeur and car arrived at eight-thirty a.m. It was a ten o'clock arrival at the Palace and I wanted to allow plenty of time, must not be late for this one. I could take three guests. Kelly, Teresa and Nikki sat in the back, I sat in the front with Peter the driver.

The traffic was light, we were in the Mall by nine-twenty and Peter was badly in need of a pee; I needed one too.

'God only knows where we'll find one around here,' was Peter's lament. I smiled and said, 'I know one, at least I used to know one, it could still be there.' I motioned him to pull into a neat lay-by next to a small building where I got many a night's sleep in my other life.

Twenty-odd years had made the place look different. It was with great relief that I rounded a line of bushes and saw the sign 'Gents Toilet' and amusement also at the sight that greeted me. A line of men, like me, immaculately dressed in morning suits, all in urgent need.

Buckingham Palace was all it should be, and more. I had been issued with a square pink sticker with a letter F on the front that was to be fixed on to the inside of the windscreen showing out. As we drove the last hundred yards towards the palace unsure quite where to go, a policewoman stepped forward and indicated a route already set into lanes. We followed gratefully, any panic that might have existed receding. From then on everything was arranged with military precision.

Guests to the left, recipients to the right. I followed a wide walkway and just as I thought I was all alone, I rounded a corner and a charming, smiling face and confident voice guided me in the right direction. Finally I arrived at the picture gallery where an increasing number of men and women were gathering, looking nervous and fidgety, even overawed, though justifiably proud.

The investitures were performed alphabetically and we moved forward slowly in groups of twelve or so. Soon I stood two from the rear of fifteen. I now felt strangely calm. I had arranged everything that I was going to do in my head in the same way I used to rehearse my act before I went on stage. Above all else I did not want to look back on this day with any regrets of thoughts or acts undone. I had a list of people I had memorised I was going to think of as I walked forward, awaiting my turn to approach the dais. I thought of Old Tom, Harry Hat, Corky and Tipperary, Mavis and David Carter and baby Susan, Mad Fred and Joanne Burton. I looked up at some of the world's most beautiful and valuable paintings that had gazed back down at generations of royalty, and remembered a man who died in a bail hostel.

'I think we had better move along if you don't mind.' A smiling man behind me pointed at a five-yard gap that had opened up between me and the recipient in front.

'I'm so sorry,' I stuttered and made up the ground.

A lady usher came towards me smiling. 'You looked miles away,' she said kindly.

'Yes, I was just thinking of . . .' I looked at her velvet suit and decided she would not understand about Jacob Jones.

Ten yards to go, I imagined my mother's smile, my father stood by her grave as I made my promise, my sister as a little girl, Nikki weighing six stone, and now she was in the palace ballroom. Teresa would be next to her and I thought of the good and not so good times we had shared. Then I imagined Kelly and the look of pride that would be on her face and I put her together with a picture I had seen of her mum, so they could enjoy the moment together in spirit.

'NICHOLAS CHARLES – FOR SERVICES TO PEOPLE WITH ALCOHOL PROBLEMS.'

I walked forward calmly and enjoyed every step with not a nerve in my body. One final thought I had to remember. In the pocket of my morning-suit jacket was an old picture of the last bed I had slept in at the Salvation Army. Prince Charles would not know that. I smiled at the irony and forced myself to remember the nights sleeping rough as I turned and bowed at his Royal Highness.

I was truly amazed at how much he knew about me – someone had done their homework well.

'Yours is a very difficult job, Mr Charles.'

'Yes, sir,' I replied. 'Nevertheless it gives me great pleasure to see the successes go back to full-time employment,' I added.

'Do you sometimes have to give them a bit of a push?' he asked.

'More of a shove,' I replied. He touched my left arm in a gesture of genuine warmth at the humour and we both laughed heartily. For a moment his face took on a serious look. 'Of course there is a great deal of tragedy caused by alcohol,' he said sombrely. I agreed as he pinned on my medal. 'Congratulations,' he said. 'You have worked extraordinarily hard for your award.'

I stepped back, bowed, his right cheek flickered a brief smile and I walked away from the dais.

Finally, the last recipients received their awards and we rejoined our families and friends and walked down the stairs from the ballroom.

'Don't forget the BBC have a camera crew waiting outside for you,' Teresa said reverting to her business management role.

This really did appeal to my sense of humour. There were many famous people at the ceremony, but only one camera crew, and they were there for me. People kept asking Nikki, Teresa and Kelly in turn. 'Who is he? What has he achieved?' I don't know all the answers they gave, but I heard Teresa say, 'You wouldn't believe me if I told you.'

I had one final act to perform. I sought out the BBC camera director and told her I was going back with my medal to Charing Cross Viaduct, or Hungerford Bridge as it is generally known nowadays. 'We'll meet you there,' she said.

I stood at the bottom of Northumberland Avenue on the corner where it meets the viaduct, an area that was once cardboard city. I had stood, sat and lain almost on the same spot in a state of filth no animal would allow itself to get into, for weeks on end and not cared. Now, resplendent in top hat and morning-suit I began to feel extremely self-conscious. I suddenly became aware of an old dosser looking in my direction from where he stood by a nearby phone box. I stared back, he looked vaguely familiar. 'Do I know you?' I asked.

'I bin 'ere since fifty-nine,' he said, 'this used to be cardboard city. Used to 'ose us down in the morning if we were late waking 'cause we drunk too much.'

'Yes, I remember,' I replied.

'You?' He looked closer. Suddenly he saw through the years. 'I know you, you're Brummie Nick.' The tears were running, I was looking at him through puddles.

'You're Bob aren't you?' I cried.

'Yes,' he said, 'I'm Bob.'

We threw our arms around one another and I rushed him back to the chauffeur, Jaguar and the girls. 'This is my old mate Bob,' I blubbered. Teresa took a photo. Passers-by couldn't believe their eyes.

Bob and I walked back to the archways, now designer shops, arm-in-arm with tears still streaming down my face. 'Are you happy?' I asked him.

'I've never known anything else, I came here when my girlfriend dumped me, I was only twenty.' He looked sad but only for a second. 'Do you remember when I got knocked over by a car and all you lot somehow got into the 'ospital to visit me? The bloody ward sister nearly 'ad a fit. They 'ad to fumigate the place, closed the ward for two nights. Tea Leaf brought me four rotten oranges off the ground at Spitalfields veg market and a bottle of meths.' We laughed like drains and more folks gave us funny looks.

'I'm sorry that I cried, I just couldn't help it,' I said pathetically. 'I've got to go now, but I'll come back to see you.'

He looked at me steadily. 'No you won't.' There was no anger in his tone. 'You won't come back 'cause you gotta keep going forward, you're all we've got, you gotta do what none of us

192

could do, you're all we got left.'

Bob turned and walked away.

'Sorry about the tears,' I yelled after him.

'You were always bloody crying in them days,' he shouted back.

He stopped and turned to face me and waved and smiled.

'Some things never change do they?' I said wiping my tears.

He thought for a moment and then spoke slowly because, now he was crying.

'One thing's changed,' he said. 'One of us has made it to the Palace.'

Epilogue

Through alcoholism and my fight for sobriety, I have met hundreds of interesting and fascinating people – I have rubbed shoulders with the rich and famous, murderers, rapists and some of the finest conmen imaginable and, as documented, a number who would have cut a throat for a pound or less and did just that.

Alcoholism has no respect for financial position or social standing and the alcoholic battlefield is littered with corpses of those who thought they had not got it. Somehow, and I imagine through the grace of God, I survived to tell the tale in this book and go on to spread the word of the glory that is sobriety through the Chaucer Clinic.

I look back across the black expanse of my late teens and twenties and see it as a remarkable apprenticeship which qualified me to lead the intensive crusade at Chaucer. I am proud to have been selected by the author of the 'Great Plan' to spread the word of my experiences and help others. More, I feel privileged to be able to offer a helping hand to those victims distraught, and to others the gift of life.

He will wipe away all tears from their eyes.
There will be no more death, no more grief or
  crying or pain.
The old things have disappeared.

Revelations 21:4